at the
dangerous edge
of social justice

Also by Thomas Fensch . . .

... and others

at the
dangerous edge

of social
justice

race, violence
and death
in America

----

thomas fensch

ISBN 978-0-9832296-6-7 hardcover
ISBN 978-0-9832296-7-4 trade paperback

New Century Books
8821 Rockdale Rd.
N. Chesterfield, Va., 23236
Newcentbks@gmail.com

Typesetting by Jill Ronsley, www.suneditwrite.com

The author is grateful to the following individuals and firms
which have granted rights to reprint copyrighted material:

Material from The Los Angeles Times reprinted with permission;
Material by Ray Sprigle courtesy of The Pittsburgh Post-Gazette;
Material by Geoffrey R. Stone, reprinted with permission;
and thanks to Dr. M. Thomas Inge for the title.

for W. Franklin Evans, Ph.D.
a brilliant and compassionate educator,
a fine friend

Contents

Prologue ...

90 AND NINE ...

There could easily be 90 and nine ...

Or 900 and 99 more individuals, widely known, half-forgotten or simply unknown, now lost to history, who risked their lives or lost their lives fighting for social justice: Ida Wells; Harriet Tubman (Aramita Harriet Ross); Sojourner Truth (Isabella Baumfree); Frederick Douglass (Frederick Augustus Washington Bailey); the Scottsboro Boys; Ralph Abernathy and others in Martin Luther King, Jr.'s inner circle; the murders of civil rights workers James Chaney, Michael Schwerner and Andrew Goodman; James Meredith; John Lewis, and a host of ministers, pastors, social activists, writers, friends, spouses, eager co-workers and sometimes co-conspirators, of the individuals in this book.

This, then, is a searing indictment of reprehensible—and often murderous—racist behavior, and a tribute to those who had courage to confront hatred, knowing full well the cost.

We could begin much earlier, but one logical beginning is Mark Twain's Huck Finn ...

One |

Huck Finn
on the Mississippi

"All right, then, I'll go to hell ..."
—Huckleberry Finn

"ALL MODERN LITERATURE COMES from one book by Mark Twain called *Huckleberry Finn* ..." Ernest Hemingway once said. "... it's the best book we've had. All American writing comes from that. There was nothing before. There has been nothing as good since."

Critic Lionel Trilling said: "It is (Twain's) masterpiece, and perhaps he learned to know that. But he could scarcely have estimated it for what it is, one of the world's great books and one of the central documents of American culture."

William Faulkner said simply that Mark Twain was "the Father of American Literature."

Samuel Langhorne Clemens was born in Florida, Missouri, scarcely a flyspeck on the map, November 30, 1835. He was four when the family moved to Hannibal, on the Mississippi. And, although he left Hannibal and traveled extensively throughout the world, figuratively he never left Hannibal; it served as the locale for *The Adventures of Tom Sawyer* and *Adventures of Huckleberry Finn*, thinly disguised as St. Petersburg.

His brother Orion owned the *Hannibal Journal* and Sam'l began as a printer's apprentice, setting type; he quickly began contributing articles and brief sketches.

He became an itinerant printer at 18, working in New York City, Philadelphia, St. Louis and Cincinnati, picking up the local culture at each stop. Like Lincoln, who "read the law" by himself, Clemens became largely self-educated at local libraries in each city.

He returned to the midwest and during a voyage down the Mississippi, he was encouraged to become a riverboat pilot. Being a pilot, he was told, was an even higher calling than being a captain; the pilot needed to know each bend, current and hazard of 2,000 miles of the Mississippi. He received his pilot's license in 1859. And eventually "found" his pseudonym, surely one of the most famous pen-names throughout literature.

Mark Twain was the call that signified two fathoms, or 12 feet of water; deep enough to be safe to navigate. He happily "borrowed it" from a previous owner, Captain Isaiah Sellers and told the story in *Life on the Mississippi,* published in 1883:

The old gentleman was not of literary turn or capacity, but he used to jot down brief paragraphs of plain, practical information about the river, and signed them "MARK TWAIN," and give them to the New Orleans *Picayune*. They related to the stage and condition of the river, and were accurate and valuable; and thus far they contained no poison. But in speaking of the stage of the river to-day at a given point, the captain was pretty apt to drop in a little remark about this being the first time he had seen the water so high or so low at that particular point in forty-nine years; and now and then he would mention Island so-and-so, and follow it, in parenthesis, with some such observation as "disappeared in 1807, if I remember rightly." In these antique interjections lay poison and bitterness for the old pilots and they used to chaff the "Mark Twain" paragraphs with unsparing mockery.

It so chanced that one of these paragraphs became the text for my first newspaper article. I burlesqued it broadly, very broadly, stringing my fantastics out to the extent of eight hundred or a thousand words. I was a "cub" at the time. I showed my performance to some pilots, and they eagerly rushed it into print in the New Orleans *True Delta*. It was a great pity; for it did nobody any worthy service and it sent a pang deep into a good man's heart. There was no malice in my rubbish; but it laughed at the captain.

It laughed at a man to whom such a thing was new and strange and dreadful. I did not know then, though I do now, that there is no suffering comparable with that which a private person feels when he is for the first time pilloried in print.

Captain Sellers did me the honor to profoundly detest me from that day forth. When I say he did me the honor, I am not using empty words. It was a very real honor to be in the thoughts of so great man as Captain Sellers and I had wit enough to appreciate it and be proud of it. It was distinction to be loved by such a man; but it was much greater distinction to be hated by him, because he loved scores of people; but he didn't sit up nights to hate anyone but me.

He never printed another paragraph while he lived, and he never again signed "Mark Twain" to anything. At the time that the telegraph brought the news of his death, I was on the Pacific coast. I was a fresh, new journalist, and needed a *nom de guerre*; so I confiscated the ancient mariner's discarded one, and have done my best to make it remain what it was in his hands—a sign and symbol and warranty that whatever is found in its company may be gambled on as being the petrified truth. How I have succeeded, it would not be modest in me to say.

And thus Mark Twain was born.

When the Civil War began, travel on the Mississippi became impossible; his time as a riverboat pilot was over. Clemens enlisted in a small Confederate unit for all of two weeks then abandoned the field; he traveled to the Nevada territory (Nevada had not yet become a state) with his brother Orion, who had taken a position as secretary to the Nevada territorial Governor James W. Nye.

Clemens became a miner in Silver City, Nevada; everywhere he went he collected memories, anecdotes, impressions, dialogue and mental sketches of the locals. His first real fame came with the publication of the short story "The Celebrated Jumping Frog of Calaveras County," in 1865, a tale he had heard in the mining camps. His adventures in the west were eventually published as *Roughing It*, in 1872.

He subsequently toured the Hawaiian islands, returned to California and began lecturing, which also made him famous.

He published his first book, *The Innocents Abroad*, in 1869 married Olivia Langdon in 1870, published *Roughing It* in 1872, *The Gilded Age* in 1873 and *The Adventures of Tom Sawyer* in 1876.

A Tramp Abroad was published in 1880, *The Prince and the Pauper* in 1882 and *Life on the Mississippi* in 1883.

He had called on his Hannibal days for *Tom Sawyer*, and then returned to it for *Adventures of Huckleberry Finn* (the *The* in the title was initially omitted). It was a satire on the mores and culture of the 1860s and dealt with the problem of slavery. He worked on it, put it away and then came back to it. What did he remember about slavery in Hannibal? He remembered well enough.

In *The Making of Mark Twain*, John Lauber writes:

> Beneath the whites were the blacks. Slavery was unquestioned: "the wise, and the good and the holy," Mark Twain recalled in his *Autobiography*, unanimously held that the institution was righteous and sacred, "the peculiar pet of the deity, and a condition which the slave himself ought to be daily and nightly thankful for." No one, at least to young Sam's knowledge, "seemed conscious that slavery was a bald, grotesque, and unwarrantable assumption." Doubters would have kept silent in any case; in the rural Missouri of the 1840s or 50s, to criticize slavery would have been to invite lynching. Denying the existence of God would have been safer. John Clemens apparently had no qualms about the institution; in 1841 he served on a jury that sentenced three abolitionists to prison terms of twelve years each for inciting slaves to escape. Mark Twain would observe, from his own experience, that it was a mistake to say that slavery made Southern whites hardhearted in general: it "merely stupefied everybody's humanity as regarded the slave." He had evidence for that in his own boyhood home. The Clemenses owned one slave—a girl named Jennie—during Sam's early childhood, and he remembered once seeing his father beat her with a bridle for insolence; Judge Clemens

cuffed, too, the small black boy whom they hired from his master "for any little blunder or awkwardness," and occasionally gave him a lashing: "which terrified the poor thing nearly out of his wits." Yet John Clemens was otherwise a humane man.

There were no great plantations nearby, and slavery as Sam knew it was of the "mild domestic variety." Yet the reality could not be avoided. Like every Southern town, Hannibal had its despised "nigger-trader"—he made a convenience scapegoat—and once Sam saw "a dozen black men and women, chained together waiting for shipment to a Southern slave market." Harsh brutality was frowned on by decent whites but could not be prevented. Mark Twain would not forget "the slave man who was struck down with a chunk of slag for some small offense; I saw him die." Once the corpse of a slave, drowned while trying to escape and then "much mutilated" by his white pursuers, rose out of the river to terrify Sam and his friends. Although a reward was offered, one of the Blankenships had kept the man's hiding place secret all summer and occasionally brought him food - behavior that Twain must have recalled when he had Huck decide to help Nigger Jim escape.

The two races were in intimate, daily contact, and white and black children could, almost, be comrades. Mark Twain could remember that he "was playmate to all the niggers, preferring their society to that of the elect." But "complete fusion" could not occur: "color and condition imposed a subtle line"—subtle, yet a barrier that not even children could ever shut out of consciousness. Sam Clemens accepted slavery, as boys do accept the basic institutions of their society: he grew up with all the unquestioned prejudices of the Southern white and even served briefly in a Confederate militia unit at the outbreak of the Civil War.

Then having left the south forever, he became aware, over the years, of his attitudes and worked to change them, doing his part to pay the debt that he came to feel every white man owed to every black man. He helped to finance the studies of a black artist in Paris and to pay the way of a black student through Yale Law School; he urged President Garfield to retain the black leader Frederick Douglass as Marshal of the District of Columbia; he read and lectured in black churches, and in his old age composed "The United States of Lyncherdom," a searing indictment of the moral cowardice by which the decent majority permitted lynching.

Adventures of Huckleberry Finn was deliberately written in *patois*; in the backwater dialects of Missouri. Dialects, plural. Twain writes in a "Explanatory":

> In this book a number of dialects are used, to wit: the Missouri negro dialect; the extremest form of the backwoods Southwestern dialect;

the ordinary "Pike County" dialect; and four modified varieties of this last. The shadings have not been done in a haphazard fashion, or by guesswork; but painstakingly, and with the trustworthy guidance and support of personal familiarity with these several forms of speech.

I made this explanation for the reason that without it many readers would suppose that all these characters were trying to talk alike and not succeeding.

In any novel that involves a trip or journey for the participants, it's not the trip that is crucial; it's the insights, the maturity or growing self-awareness along the way, or any epiphanies that the participants discover, that are the keys.

John Steinbeck's *The Grapes of Wrath*, published in 1939 during the depths of the Great Depression is a prime example.

When the Joads are forced off their farm in Oklahoma, 12 of them pile into an ancient truck and head to California, which had been touted as a western paradise. They discover they are treated far more savagely in California then they ever had been in Oklahoma, called "Okies" and despised. At the novel's end, the family unit is fractured; the grandparents had died and others—including Tom Joad, who was something of a prodigal son—had disappeared, but the remaining members believe they are wise enough and strong enough to survive.

The epiphany in *Huckleberry Finn* occurs when Huck and Jim are floating down the Mississippi on a raft, as free as they can expect to be. (There is no thought to the idea if, somehow, they had gone *upstream*, they may have reached a Free State or somehow gotten nigger Jim into the Underground Railroad to safety. They are floating downstream, deeper and deeper into the vicious heart of the segregated south.)

Huck knows that by law and custom he should return Jim to his rightful owner. In chapter 31, with the apt title "You Can't Pray a Lie," Huck says:

> At last I had an idea; and I says, I'll go and write the letter—and *then* see if I can pray. Why, it was astonishing, the way I felt as light as a feather right straight off, and my troubles all gone. So I got a piece of paper and a pencil, all glad and excited, and set down and wrote:

> Miss Watson, your runaway nigger Jim is down here two miles below Pikesville, and Mr. Phelps has got him and he will give him up for the reward you send. HUCK FINN

> I felt good and all washed clean of sin for the first time I had ever felt so in my life, and I knowed I could pray now. But I didn't do it straight off, but laid the paper down and set there thinking—thinking how good it was all this happened so, and how near I come to being lost and going to hell. And when on thinking. And got to thinking over our trip down the river; and I see Jim before me all the time: in the day and in the night-time, sometimes

moonlight, sometimes storms, and we a-floating along, talking and singing and laughing. But somehow I couldn't seem to strike no places to harden me against him, but only the other kind. I'd see him standing my watch on top of his'n, 'stead of calling me, so I could go on sleeping; and see how glad he was when I come back out of the fog; and when I come to him again in the swamp, up there where the feud was; and such-like times; and would always call me honey, and pet me, and do everything he could think of for me and how good he always was; and at least I struck the time I saved him by telling the men we had smallpox aboard, and he was so grate-ful, and said I was the best friend old Jim ever had in the world, and the *only* one he he's got now; and then I happened to look and see that piece of paper.

It was a close place. I took it up, and held it in my hand. I was a trembling, because I'd got to decide, forever, betwixt two things, and I knowed it. I studied a minute, sort of holding my breath, and says to myself:

"All right, then I'll go to hell," and tore it up.

It was awful thoughts and awful words, but they was said. And I let them stay said ....

This was, of course, Clemens/Twain speaking through the perceptions and thoughts of an uneducated boy, scarcely no more than 13 or 14 at the time.

In *Bookbanning in America: Who Bans Books? And Why*, William Noble writes:

When he wrote *The Adventures of Huckleberry Finn* in 1885, Mark Twain knew he would be tweaking Victorian morality. His characters and situations repelled a conventional work ethic and wisdom gained though formal education. His heros were not high born, yet they tantalized with their sense of adventure and their underdog role in a life harsher than most readers know.

Many were attractive rogues and criminals, often speaking with fractured syntax and in street vernacular: others—particularly the runaway slave Jim—spoke in crude misstatement but offered insights and judgments both accurate and humorous. Mark Twain knew his characters would offend, because he understood the conventional morality that would judge his book.

Because of the phrase *nigger Jim*, which occurs regularly throughout the text, Twain knew that the book would be controversial.

(That word *nigger*, was of course, common during the Civil War, especially the slave states; Twain's book was published scarcely 20 years later, in 1885, when old wounds and animosities were still raw. In some editions, a century and more past the original publication, *nigger Jim* has been replaced by *slave Jim* and, in one edition, *hipster Jim*. None of these variants have been successful. In 1879, just a few years before Twain published *Huckleberry Finn*, Joseph Conrad published *The Nigger of the 'Narcissus': a Tale of the Sea*. The

American edition was titled *The Children of the Sea* because publisher Dodd, Mead thought readers would not buy a book about a black man, or buy a book with the word *nigger* in the title. In 2009, the WordBridge Publishing company issued an edition with the improbable title *The N-Word of the Narcissus*.)

William Noble also writes:

> In 1885, the public library in Concord, Massachusetts, banned *Huckleberry Finn*, finding it course, crude and inelegant. "Trash suitable only for the slums," was the view. Instead of hanging his head in shame, Twain actually rejoiced because he could see that his condemnation in this tight-minded Puritan stronghold would add allure to the book elsewhere. His disposition grew positively radiant when Louisa May Alcott, that proper author of proper novels such as *Little Women*, couldn't resist a public comment. "If Mr. Clemens cannot think of something better to tell our pure-minded lads and lasses," she wrote, "he had best stop writing for them."
>
> Ah, Mark Twain must have thought, such a gift! Slyly, he didn't tell the truth about *Huckleberry Finn*: the book was not selling, few people wanted to buy it; this new story from the pen of the great Twain caught readers between yawns.
>
> A spark from the Concord Public Library changed all. Two weeks after the banning Twain wrote a letter to his nephew Charles Webster,

who happened to be his publisher (he co-owned the publishing company with Webster):

Dear Charley;

 The Committee of the Public Library of Concord Mass., have given us a rattling tip-off puff which will go into every paper in the country. They have expelled Huck from their library ...

 Many authors would have been incensed—how dare they!—But the great Twain understood that immutable law of political success: the more a thing is mentioned, the more important it became.

 Until it became essential. He added a final line to his nephew:

 "That will sell 25,000 copies for us sure."

Actually his prediction was modest. Within two months of the banning, *The Adventures of Huckleberry Finn* sold more than 50,000 copies.

In *Mr. Clemens and Mark Twain*, published in 1966, Justin Kaplan wrote:

> In time *Huckleberry Finn* would be read in ten million copies printed in every tongue and nobody would question its rank in literature.

And surely it has surpassed ten million copies today.

Two |

Lumpkin's Jail, Richmond, Virginia

"... the classroom windows still had their prison bars, and the former whipping posts were used as lecterns for the professors."
—Raymond Hylton

THIS IS A HISTORY of both a figurative *and* literal descent into savage depravity and a triumph of the human spirit.

David Zucchino told some of the story in his article "With unearthing of infamous jail, Richmond confronts its slave past," published in the *Los Angeles Times,* December 18, 2008:

> RICHMOND, VA.—The place called Lumpkin's Slave Jail was indeed a jail, but it was much more than that. It was a holding pen for human chattel.

In Richmond's Shockoe Bottom river district, the notorious slave trader Robert Lumpkin ran the city's largest slave-holding facility in the 1840s and 1950s. Tens of thousands of blacks were held in the cramped brick building while they waited to be sold.

Those who refused were publicly whipped.

"The individual would be laid down, his hands and feet stretched out and fastened in the rings, and a great big man would stand over him and flog him," a clergyman wrote after witnessing the punishment.

On Wednesday, black and white Richmond residents walked together across the rain-slicked cobblestones, excavated this month, that mark the outlines of the old slave jail. This former Confederate capital's announcement that Lumpkin's Jail had been found was the latest acknowledgment of its painful slave history.

Since Richmond's City Council formed the Slave Trail Commission in 1998, the city gradually has been confronting both the enslavement of blacks and their contribution to the city.

"This is a part of our history that was covered up too long," said Charles Vaughan, a retired bus operator and commission member.

A descendant of slaves, Vaughan stood staring at the jail's spectral remains Wednesday, wondering whether some distant relative once was imprisoned there.

Richmond, which is 57 percent black, long has honored its Confederate past with monuments to Gen. Robert E. Lee, President Jefferson Davis and thousands of rebel soldiers. But only with its decade-long examination of the slave trail—which includes the jail, an adjoining Negro Burial Ground, and the slave marketplace and docks—has it shone a light on its legacy of slavery.

"It was hushed for so long," said Ana Edwards, of the Sacred Ground Project, which erected a historical marker for the cemetery, which is covered by a university parking lot. "Slavery was not something anybody wanted to address."

Blacks called Lumpkin's Slave Jail "Devils Half Acre." Some died there from abuse and disease. Thousands more were fed and groomed for sale at nearby slave markets, then sent by boat or rail to toil on farms and plantations throughout the South.

"There were literally sold down the river," said Philip J. Schwartz, a professor emeritus at Virginia Commonwealth University, standing a few feet from the jail site and gesturing toward the nearby James River.

From 1808, when the United States outlawed the international slave trade, to the end of the Civil War, an estimated 300,000 slaves were sold in Richmond. Lumpkin, known as a "bully trader" for his harsh treatment of slaves, sold the men, women and children who became slaves in Southern states, where slavery remained legal.

Archaeologists discovered that Lumpkin's jail was actually a complex of brick buildings.

(The Shockoe Bottom area is one of the lowest areas in Richmond and Robert Lumpkin's slave jail building was even lower than other buildings in his complex. Thus approaching the jail building downward was literally a descent into depravity. Discovery of the Lumpkin's Jail area has been hindered by water constantly seeping into excavations from the nearby James River.) David Zucchino also writes:

In addition to the 20-by-41-foot, two-story jail, there was a kitchen, Lumpkin's residence and boarding house where antebellum slave owners stayed while their slaves were readied for sale.

Digging through 15 feet of muck and fill dirt beneath a city-owned parking lot, archaeologists unearthed cobblestones and brick drains that former the jail's perimeter.

The jail was torn down in the 1870s.

"We are standing in a time capsule of Richmond's history," Matthew Laird, an archaeologist on the dig, said as he led commission members across the water-logged site. "It's exciting to find such an intact and well-preserved site."

The discovery of the jail continues the city's "public acknowledgment of Richmond's enslaved African Americans," said Delores L. McQuinn, City Council vice president and chairwoman of the Slave Trail Commission.

"Many of us here were trying to work through this without the facts," McQuinn said. She was referring to fellow African American commission members who came of age when Richmond's white leadership ignored the contributions of slaves and their descendants on the city's past.

Because of the Slave Trail and the commemoration of "this infamous jail," McQuinn said, "generations to come won't have to do as much work to find out who they are and where they came from."

Kathleen Kilpatrick, director of the state Department of Historical Resources, said the jail has national significance. She called it "ground zero" for understanding the slave trade.

David Herring, who heads a local historical conservation group, said the slave trade and the city are inextricably linked: "Richmond would not be here without the slaves that built this city."

The jail site is steeped in slavery's history. Near the jail was a city gallows where Gabriel Prosser, who led a 1800 slave revolt known as Gabriel's Rebellion, was executed.

On auction blocks nearby, the family of Henry "Box" Brown was sold to a North Carolina plantation owner. According to some accounts, Brown escaped a similar fate by packing himself into a wooden crate labeled "dry goods" that was shipped to Philadelphia and freedom.

When Robert Lumpkin died, he left his jail to his widow—Mary Lumpkin, a black woman and former slave. In 1867, she gave the property to a minister to established a school for freed blacks.

Over the years, the school evolved into what is now Virginia Union University, a historically black college.

In another article, titled "Digging Up the Past at a Richmond Jail," published in the *Smithsonian* magazine, March 2009, Abigail Tucker wrote that Lumpkin had five children with his common-law wife, Mary. Tucker quoted professor Philip Schwartz, who said Lumpkin was "both an evil man and a family man."

... Lumpkin sent two of his mixed-race daughters to finishing school in Massachusetts. According to Charles Henry Corey, a former Union chaplain, Lumpkin later sent the girls and their mother to live in the free state of Pennsylvania, concerned that a "financial contingency might arise when these, his own beautiful daughters, might be sold into slavery to pay his debts."

... an evil man ... a family man ...

Lumpkin was concerned that a ... *"financial contingency might arise when these, his own beautiful daughters, might be sold into slavery to pay his debts."*

The end paragraph of the David Zucchino *Los Angeles Times* article is very much an understated coda. There is much more to this history than the end of the Civil War in Richmond. Abigail Tucker wrote:

Lumpkin was in Richmond in April, 1865, when the city fell to Union soldiers. Shackling some 50 enslaved and weeping men, women and children together, the trader tried to board a train heading south, but there was no room. He died not long after the war ended.

In 1867, a Baptist minister named Nathaniel Colver was looking for a space for the black seminary he hoped to start. After a day of prayer, he set out into the city's streets, where he met Mary "in a group of colored people," recalling her as a "large, fair-faced freedwoman, nearly white, who said *she* had a place which she thought I could have."

That chance meeting between Mary Lumpkin and Nathaniel Colver quickly led to a remarkable story.

A *most* remarkable story.

Nathaniel Colver needed rooms to establish a school for freed blacks. Mary Lumpkin had rooms available—in the former slave jail.

Although Abigail Tucker's *Smithsonian* article says the bars were taken down from the windows before Lumpkin's Jail was leased to Colver, Virginia Union University History professor (and University historian) Raymond Hylton has written, "the classroom windows still had their prison bars and the former whipping posts were used as lecterns for the professors."

But Colver was over 70 and, in 1868, his place was taken by Dr. Charles Henry Corey. In 1870, the school purchased the former United States Hotel building in downtown Richmond for $10,000. In 1876, the school, first called the Colver Institute, was renamed the Richmond Institute; the name was changed again in 1886 to the Richmond Theological Seminary.

In the 1890s, the campus was moved to Lombardy Street in the near northeast downtown area: nine matching granite buildings in Victorian Romanesque style were constructed; five are still well-maintained and in continuous use today.

In 1899, it merged with another fledging school, Wayland Seminary, to form Virginia Union University.

Hartshorn Memorial College were merged with Virginia Union University in 1932 and, in 1964, Storer College, of Harper's Ferry, West Virginia, also merged with Virginia Union—thus four schools have come together in the past.

On February, 22, 1960, 34 Virginia Union University students staged a sit-in at Thalhimer's department store's segregated dining facilities in downtown Richmond. All were arrested for "trespassing." Dr. Allix James, then Dean of the University's School of Theology, and who later became the University's President (1970-1979), put up his home as bail collateral for all 34. The NAACP and the Virginia Union University chapter of Alpha Kappa Alpha sorority also contributed to the bail funds needed.

At the local courts level, all of the Richmond 34 were found guilty, but the verdicts were appealed. The case moved upward through the legal system. The Supreme Court agreed to hear the case and, at the level of the Supreme Court, the Richmond 34 won. The arrest of the "Richmond 34" was the first mass arrest of the modern Civil Rights movement. Racial segregation was eliminated in Virginia within two years.

Virginia Union University will celebrate its 150th year of continuous operation in 2015; it is one of the oldest historically black universities in the United States.

Virginia Union University's motto, translated from the Latin is: *God will provide.* And it has never forgotten its heritage: *it began in a slave jail.*

Three |

1948: Ray Sprigle

Into a Black World ...

RAY SPRIGLE IS NOW one of the forgotten names in Civil Rights history. John Howard Griffin's *Black Like Me* has now been read by millions world-wide since its first publication over 50 years ago and is still in print. Many assume Griffin's remarkable odyssey through the segregated south was the first of its kind; in fact, it was the second.

Ray Sprigle was first.

Sprigle's name was not exactly unknown in the newspaper world before his trip into the land of Jim Crow. His stories of Supreme Court judge Hugo Black's connection with the Klu Klux Klan won him the Pulitzer Prize in 1938, and in 1944 the Headliner's Club, a journalism-based civic association in Austin, Texas, presented him a medal for his series about the black market in meat. He dug out the information for the series by posing as a black-market butcher. Similarly, he took a job as an attendant in several state institutions, while gathering material for a series on Pennsylvania's hospitals in 1947 and worked as a coal miner for another story.

Previously, Sprigle attended Ohio State University for one year and left. He took a job with the now long-defunct *Ohio Sun* in Columbus, then, as was the custom, became something of a newspaper vagabond, working on ten different midwestern newspapers, some for only a few days, some for as much as a year. He did take a longer job at the *Pittsburgh Post*, working his way up to city editor, but preferred writing and so returned to that.

Sprigle wrote a series of articles for the *Pittsburgh Post-Gazette* in 1948, which were first released in pamphlet for under the title "I Was a Negro in the South for Thirty Days" and which was subsequently published in book form by Simon & Schuster in 1949 under the (better) title, *In the Land of Jim Crow*.

It was a remarkable exercise in deception, aided by Walter White, executive director of the National Association for the Advancement of Colored People, and John Wesley Dobbs, who traveled with him during the four-week trek. Sprigle has to learn to be black; Dobbs could aid him (and help protect him if necessary). Later, John Howard Griffin had no such support. When Griffin dyed his skin black, he had to learn practically instantly how to think and behave like a black man. Sprigle had help. (Sprigle got a three-week suntan in Florida before his trip; with papers indicating he was black, he simply *said* he was black.) In the first article in his series, Sprigle writes:

I was a Negro in the Deep South.

Now I, a "white" man, know, as well as any white man may, what it means to be a black man below the Mason-Dixon line—the Smith and Wesson line to us black folk.

For four endless, fear-filled weeks, along with my ten million other Negroes of the South, I lived under the burden of the Jim Crow system, with its iniquitous pattern of oppression and cruelty and discrimination.

I ate, slept, traveled, lived black. I lodged in Negro households. I ate in Negro restaurants. I crept through the back and side doors of railroad and bus stations. I traveled Jim Crow in trains and buses and streetcars and taxicabs. It was a strange, new—and for me, uncharted—world that I entered when, in a Jim Crow railroad coach, we rumbled across the Potomac out of Washington. It was a world of which I had no remote conception, despite scores of trips through the South. The world I had known in the South was white. Now I was black and the world I was to know was as bewildering as if I had been dropped down on the moon.

The towers and turrets of the great cities of the Southland, painted against the falling night as we rolled along, represented a civilization and an economy almost completely alien to me and the rest of the black millions in the South.

Only twice in my month-long sojourn was my status as a black man even remotely questioned. A Negro doctor in Atlanta, to whom I was introduced and with whom I talked briefly, later turned to my Negro companion, who was leading me along the unfamiliar paths of the world of color and demanded "What are you carrying that white man around with you for?"

To which my friend replied, "He says he's a Negro and that's enough for me. Have you found any way of telling who carries Negro blood and who doesn't?" And if the doctor wasn't convinced, he was at least silenced.

Another time when my membership in the black race was doubted was my own fault. I broke my resolution to keep my mouth shut. For a couple of days I was alone in Atlanta, living in the Negro YMCA and eating in a small but excellent restaurant. Mrs. Hawk, the proprietress, tangled me in conversation one day—never a difficult task for anyone. So I talked too much, too fast and too expansively.

A couple of days later she met my friend and remarked: "That friend of yours—he talks too much to be a Negro. I think he's white."

But in literally thousands of contacts with Negroes, from nationally known leaders of the race to sharecroppers in the cotton rows, I was accepted as a Negro. I sat for long hours in Negro groups where we discussed everything from Shakespeare to atomic energy and the price of cotton. Neither I nor my companion ever detected any reserve or suspicion that I wasn't just what I pretended to be, a light-skinned Negro from Pittsburgh, down south on a visit.

I attended a half a dozen Negro meetings, from YMCA banquets to political conferences and church gatherings, and was even called upon to speak.

My contacts with whites were few indeed, but here too, I went unsuspected and unquestioned. Southern whites have long taken the position that when a man says he's black, so far as they are concerned he is. So the white folks never lifted an eyebrow when I sat in the Jim Crow section of trains, buses and street cars, drank from "For Colored" fountains in courthouse and railroad stations, ate in Negro restaurants, sat in the "For Colored" sections of rail and bus stations. Rarely is a light or white Negro questioned in the South when he seeks Jim Crow accommodations. Now and then a conductor or policeman will remind a passenger, apparently a white, in a Jim Crow coach, or a light skinned Negro entering a "For Colored" restaurant, "That's for Negroes, you know." But the usual response of "I'm where I belong" ends the matter right there.

I heard of scores of instances of white-skinned Negroes—or, one should say, men with both white and black blood—being ejected from white sections of buses, streetcars or trains, usually because someone who knew them complained to the driver or conductor.

But only one incident did I hear of where a man who called himself a Negro was summarily tossed into a white railroad coach despite his insistence, "I'm where I belong."

That was when the father of a friend of mine in Atlanta boarded a Jim Crow coach in Birmingham. Both father and son could pass for white anywhere, but through choice have cast their lot with their darker brethren, as have so many thousands of Negroes with a preponderance of white blood.

"Look," admonished the conductor, "don't you know you can't ride with those niggers? It's against the law."

That was one time when the standard reply "I'm where I belong," didn't go over.

"Look here, you," rejoined the conductor, "it's fellows like you that are goin' to upset this whole damned applecart. You git up in the white coaches, and no argument." And "up in the white coaches" his passenger went.

Probably the conductor hadn't reasoned the thing out throughly, but undoubtedly he realized that, come the day when neither he nor any other white could be certain of distinguishing great numbers of Negroes from the white cousins, Old Jim Crow was in for a terrible lacing.

It took no great acumen to realize that no Northern white man, even though fairly well disguised as a Negro, could make his way through the black South alone, and completely on his own. He'd meet with suspicion and rebuff not only from whites but, more importantly, from Negroes too. So a companion, unmistakably a Negro, and familiar with every phase of the black world of the South, was inevitably the solution to that problem. For that I turned to Walter White, executive director of the National Association for the Advancement of Colored People.

Scores of times Walter White has traversed the South from end to end, posing as a white man, risking his life every mile and every minute of his journeyings. And here was a white newspaperman from Pittsburgh who wanted to reverse the process and turn Negro. The idea caught his fancy. He found the man I needed to lead me through the warrens of the black south.

And if there is any commendation due anyone for these chronicles, surely the lion's share must go to that companion of mine. I doubt if there are many men who know the south, black and white, as he does. We ate, slept, lived and traveled together for four weeks. If I learned anything about the life of the Negro, it is because he took me into the places, the men and women from whom I might learn.

We'd roll along through the night, our destination the Negro section of a town perhaps two hundred miles away, and for hours I'd listen while he recited long passages from *Macbeth*, Ingersoll's essay on Napoleon—page after page from the best in English literature. All his life he had fought against the oppression, the injustice and the discrimination weighing on his people. But there is no bitterness, no hatred in the man. To him, his "Southland," as he always calls it, is the fairest country in the land. He loves his Georgia above all other states—he would live nowhere else in America.

In four weeks and four thousand miles of travel we met and talked with hundreds of the Negro leaders of the South. If in four weeks anyone can get the actual picture of the life of the Negro in the South, then I got it. Because that friend of Walter White—and now my friend too—made it possible for me to live that life.

I became James Rayel Crawford, Negro, from Pittsburgh, come south to visit friends. I built up an identity as a not too industrious small-time writer and had the necessary papers and letters to prove it. I never got a chance to show them to anyone. Without question, I became "Brother Crawford," welcomed wherever we went with generous hospitality and heart-warming friendliness.

One last word as I begin this account of my four weeks of life as a Negro in the Deep South: Don't anybody try to tell me that the North discriminates against the Negro, too, and seek to use that as a defense against the savage oppression and the brutal intolerance the black man encounters in the South. Discrimination against the Negro in the North is an annoyance and an injustice. In the South it is bloodstained tragedy.

In the North the Negro meets with rebuff and insult when he seeks service at hotels and restaurants. But, at least in states like Pennsylvania and others, he can take his case to court and he invariably wins.

But in the South he is barred by law not only from white hotels and restaurants but from public parks and swimming pools, from many public buildings—and where he isn't barred he is restricted to "For Colored" drinking fountains, rest rooms, even elevators in many courthouses and city halls. By law he may not enter bus or railroad stations through the entrances reserved for whites. He must crawl in through a side or back door. By law he must find himself a seat in the rear of a bus and street car—or in a railroad coach—and if the white folks need the space, he doesn't get aboard at all.

His children are barred from white schools by law and are thrust into shacks in which no intelligent Northern farmer would house his pigs. White children ride to school in buses. Black ones walk. From his birth, when he's born in a Jim Crow hospital—if he's lucky enough to rate that kind of birth—until the day he dies in a Jim Crow slum, is coffined by a Jim Crow undertaker, is buried in a Jim Crow cemetery, and gets his name on a Jim Crow honor roll, he is proscribed and oppressed and abused to a degree that no Northern Negro ever heard of.

Don't anybody try to tell me anything about the lot of the Negro in the South. That much at least I know. And nobody told me. I saw it for myself.

No Northern white can deny there is is discrimination against the Negro in the North. Prejudice against the black citizen breaks out in race riots from time to time, as witness Detroit in recent years, and Chicago and Springfield, Illinois, in an earlier day. But in the North, both black and white rioters go to prison. In the South only the black ones climb the steps to a gallows or serve time in a cell.

In short, discrimination against the Negro in the North is usually in defiance of the law. In the South it is enforced and maintained by the law.

Let me make clear at the start, too, that this is no complete and impartial survey of the race problem in the South. This is the story of a newspaperman who lived as a Negro in the South and didn't like it. I deliberately sought out the worst that the South could show me in the way of discrimination and oppression of the Negro. I spent most of my time in Georgia, Mississippi and Alabama. I ignored Virginia and North Carolina, where the greatest progress in development and civilized race relations has been recorded. How can you correct evil until

you find it? I deliberately sought the evil and
the barbarous aspects of the white South's treatment of the Negro. It is of that only that I write.

The chapter titles in the book form of Sprigle's journey show the style and tone of his work:

Into a Black World
Not Quite Slavery—Not Quite Freedom
The Problem of "Passing"
Southern Hospitality—Negro style
Don't "Figure Behind the Man"
Negroes, Too, Are Different
"Justifiable Homicide in Self-Defense"
The Real Meaning of "Separate But Equal"
Jim Crow is No Humorist
Not All the World Is Dark
Never Forget You're Black
Jim Crow in Reverse
"Voters Don't Kill Easy"
Voting Is the Bright and Beautiful Dream
A Dead Man Was Voting
Fear Walks with Me
"The Man" Rules the Delta
Black Money and White Schools
"Skin Ball"
This Amazing Lost World
White Hospitals and Black Deaths
Not So Strange Bedfellows
Even in Atlanta We Die
The White Man's Ocean

More Than One Way to Skin a Voter
The Negro's Faith
Gents' Room Survey
Life, Liberty, and the Pursuit of Justice
Pastoral in Black
Crossing Back

One of most horrific stories Sprigle uncovered as a reporter was the death of Henry Gilbert in Georgia on May 29, 1947. It is chapter seven in his book, "Justifiable Homicide in Self-Defense":

> She is worn and aged and bent beyond her time. Her hands are warped and gnarled as she wrings them helplessly. Nearly a quarter of a century behind a plow and mule under blazing Georgia suns has done that to her.
>
> In a haze of dull despair, this broken, hopeless Negro farm woman sits in the drab, neat little parlor in black Atlanta and tells her tale of wanton murder. Terror and tragedy seemingly have wrung her dry of emotion.
>
> "When the white folks gave him back to me he was in his coffin. I held his head in my hands when I kissed him. And I felt the broken pieces of bone under the skin. It was just like a sackful of little pieces of bone.
>
> "I put my arms around him for one last time as he lay there. All down one side him there were no ribs—just pieces that moved when I held him."

That was her husband she was talking about—Henry Gilbert, forty-two years old, Negro farmer, murdered by the white folks of Harris and Trump Counties, Georgia, May 29, 1947.

Henry Gilbert was victim of the mores of the white Southerner. When a Negro kills a white man and escapes, another Negro—any Negro—had to pay. Henry Gilbert just happened to be the Negro picked for slaughter.

Sunday night, May 4, Olin Sands, a white planter, in his pickup truck overtook Gus Davidson, a young Negro with a bad record among both blacks and whites, driving his father's car, in front of Union Springs Baptist Church. Sands accused him of driving over a calf lying in the road and began beating the Negro with a club. The Negro shot and killed him.

Henry Gilbert, a deacon and treasurer of the little Baptist church, was inside the church counting the evening's collection. Mrs. Gilbert and the wives of the other deacons were waiting in front. At the sounds of the shots they called their menfolk and everybody started for home in short order.

Two weeks later, E.V. Hilyer, Sheriff of Troup County, with two officers from Harris County appeared at the Gilbert home at four-thirty in the morning. They arrested him on a warrant charging him with aiding and abetting the escape of Gus Davidson, despite the fact that a short time before Gilbert had had Davidson arrested and jailed for creating a disturbance in the church. Davidson, his father, Lovett Davidson, and their white employer, Luke Sturdevant, had all told Gilbert that they'd get even with him. The officers drove away with Gilbert just as it was getting light.

And that glimpse of him in the early dawn, three gun-hung white men shepherding him into their car, was the last time Carolyn Gilbert was ever to see her husband alive. "He'd be dead when the white folks gave him back."

For the next ten days Henry Gilbert dropped out of sight while Georgia law dragged him from jail to jail. Early Monday Mrs. Gilbert hurried to Hamilton. She was told her husband had been "carried" to Columbus, where "the FBI wanted to talk with him." Not until May 29 did Mrs.

Gilbert get any definite word as to where her husband was being held. That afternoon, two of her uncles, Jesse and Cicero Davenport, told her that Henry was back in Hamilton Jail, that they had talked to him through his cell window.

Friday morning, "happier than I can tell you, Mr. Crawford," at the news that her husband was alive and well, she bustled through breakfast and got ready to go to Hamilton to see the husband she feared was dead.

She was all dressed and was waiting for a neighbor to drive her into town when another neighbor, Willie B. Andrews, came in.

A white man, Mr. Louis Booker, had given Willie word to carry to Mrs. Gilbert. Her husband was dead. She'd find his body in a Hamilton undertaker's rooms.

Thursday night County Policemen Willie H. Buchanan had gone into Henry Gilbert's cell. "To get a confession," he said afterwards.

"The nigger drew a chair on me and I had to kill him."

Here is what the undertaker found when he fixed Henry Gilbert's body up for burial:

His skull was crushed to a pulp in front and in back. One leg and one arm were broken. All the ribs on one side were smashed into splinters. He was riddled by five bullets fired as close range. That is what Georgia justice officially describes as "justifiable homicide in self- defense." And Willie Buchanan, wanton killer is "man of the year" in Harris and Troup counties.

The white folks gave Carolyn Gilbert less than a month to mourn her husband in peace. Then came Sheriff Hilyer with another "aiding-abetting-escape" warrant and Carolyn went to the same jail where her husband was murdered. She was there only twenty-four hours, however, before Attorney Dan Duke, the man who smashed the Columbians, had her out on $1,000. bail.

"I just don't understand the white people," says Mrs. Gilbert. "If Henry had an enemy in the world it was Gus Davidson. He was a bad man. He came into our church with a gun and threatened one of our deacons. Henry had him jailed for that. And right then Gus Davidson told Henry he'd get even. So did his father, Lovett Davidson, and so did Lovett Davidson's white man, Luke Sturdevant."

At Mrs. Gilbert's preliminary hearing, when she was held for court, Davidson testified he had seen his fugitive son eating breakfast in the Gilbert home.

"Why, I wouldn't have let Gus Davidson sit at my table. I wouldn't have let him come into my house at any time—let alone when he was hunted for murder," declared Carolyn. Sheriff Hilyer himself pinned perjury on both Davidson and Sturdevant, but a justice of the peace held Mrs. Gilbert for trial.

Now word from Harris County is that the white folks want to drop the case against Mrs. Gilbert and just forget the whole thing. It won't make much difference to the dry- eyed huddled woman in the chair across from me. Her life is finished. And the life of Henry and Carolyn Gilbert had built out of toil and struggle through the years is finished too.

"Twenty-two years we were married before the white folks killed him," she says, not a sign of emotion in her voice. "We sharecropped two years and I worked with him in the fields from the day we were married. Then we saved enough to buy us a little old mule and we went to rentin'. We worked seventeen years on our rented farm and saved our money until we had

$1,350. So we bought us a farm a few miles out of Chipley. It was 111 acres and run down pretty bad. But we built it up, Henry and me, working from daylight to dark.

"Henry borrowed $1,000 from the man at the bank and he let Henry have it on just his note. We had the whole farm wired in. We had nine cows and four big hogs and two mules. Henry worked one of the mules and I worked the other. But we didn't let the girls work in the cotton. Henry wanted learning for them. So they all went to high school in LaGrange. Two of them go to high school here now and the other one graduated and works in Mr. Rich's store.

"Henry paid back the thousand dollars he borrowed and the bank man lent him $600. more. Henry worked on the house, too. We had five rooms—big rooms and screens on every window, and he screened in the whole back porch too."

All of this, the murder of her husband, the simple story of her life, without a tear, without a tremor in her voice.

Suddenly she dropped her head in her hands and sobs shook her.

"Every night I keep asking God to help me. But I don't know what he could do. Help me pray. Pray for me."

Me, a white man—even though she thinks I'm black—pray for Carolyn Gilbert! Who would listen?

The book version of Sprigle's trip, *In the Land of Jim Crow*, pre-dated John Howard Griffin's *Black Like Me* by more than a decade. But Griffin dyed his skin black to become a black man and in doing so, very nearly lost his own psyche. Written in the first-person "I" form, *Black Like Me* is a far more more compelling and unforgettable book; it has now been in print for over 50 years and has been published world-wide.

Sprigle died in December, 1957; *In the Land of Jim Crow* has long been out-of-print and is now largely forgotten.

Four |

1955: Emmett Till

Murdered in Mississippi August 28, 1955
Age: 14

THE MURDER OF EMMETT Till in 1955 was perhaps the first racial hate crime that engendered national *and* international condemnation and revulsion.

Over a half century after the crime, there are some facts still open to question.

Emmett Till was the son of Mamie Carthan and Louis Till. When Mamie was two her family moved from Webb, Mississippi, in the Delta, to Argo, Illinois, during a vast migration of blacks to the Chicago area and elsewhere. Argo eventually had such a large percentage of black residents it was called "little Mississippi." In the 1940s, over 214,000 blacks migrated to the Chicago area and about half came from Mississippi.

No one would question why there was a vast migration to the north. Mississippi was the poorest state in the nation in the 1950s and the Delta counties were some of the poorest in Mississippi. In Tallahatchie County, where Mamie Carthan was born, the average income per household in 1949 was $690. ($6,324 in 2010 dollars); for black families it was $462 ($4,234 in 2010 dollars). Economic opportunities for blacks were almost nonexistent. Most of them were sharecroppers who lived on land owned by whites.

Emmett Till was born July 25, 1941. His mother and father separated in 1942 after an argument: he had been unfaithful; she discovered the affair. He choked her into unconsciousness, she subsequently threw scalding water at him. After Louis Till violated a court order to stay away from Mamie, a judge ordered him to go to jail or join the Army. He enlisted in the Army in 1943.

In *Death in the Delta*, Stephen Whitfield writes:

> ... it was a terrible and grotesque coincidence ...
>
> Private Louis Till was convinced of raping two Italian women, Benni Lucrezia and Frieda Mari, and of killing a third, Anna Nanchi. These crimes were perpetrated in Civitavecchia, in June, 1944. Private Till, who was then twenty-two years old, pleaded not guilty. He was nevertheless court-martialed for violating Article of War #92 in February, 1945 and was hanged at Aversa, Italy, in July 2.

(Later there were attempts to connect Private Till's rape and murder court marshal to the Emmett Till case in Mississippi. There was no possible connection—Emmett Till did not even know his father, and nothing was made of it, except additional sordid publicity. Mamie Till knew nothing of that; she was told Louis Till was killed because of "willful misconduct.")

Emmett was largely raised solely by his mother. A bout of non-paralytic polio when he was three left him with a speech impairment; a stutter and he was said to make a whistle-like sound when he tried to talk, a factor in the subsequent encounter with Carolyn Bryant, later in Mississippi.

As he grew, Emmett was apparently good in school, something of a prankster and who, for his age, dressed well. In his wallet he carried a picture of a white girl, inconsequential in the Chicago area, but which had deadly consequences in Mississippi.

At 14, he looked—and largely acted—like an adult.

In 1955, his great-uncle, Mose Wright visited from Mississippi and told Emmett of life in the Delta; Emmett wanted to see for himself.

His mother agreed to the trip, but warned him that Chicago and Mississippi were two different worlds and he had to behave differently in front of whites in Mississippi. Emmett told her he understood.

In the evening of August 24, 1955, Till and seven other boys and one girl piled into a car and drove to Money, Mississippi, ten miles north of Greenwood. It looked like a scene from John Steinbeck's 1939 Depression-era classic, *The Grapes of Wrath*:

The town had one paved road and consisted of three stores, plus a post office, a school, a gas station and a building for ginning cotton. One of the stores, which featured a standard large Coco-Cola sign in front, specialized in selling snuff and fatback to black field hands.

The store, Bryant's Grocery and Meat Market, was owned by Roy Bryant and his wife Carolyn. When the car full of teenagers, including Emmett Till arrived, Bryant was gone, taking a load of shrimp to Texas. He left his wife with Juanita Milam, the wife of Bryant's half-brother J.W. Milam.

Emmett had been bragging about a white girlfriend he had in Chicago. And here the conversation in front of Bryant's grocery veered into tragedy. "There's a white woman inside," one of the others told Emmett. "Bet you won't go in there and talk to her."

Emmett walked into the grocery, bought two cents of bubblegum and when Carolyn Bryant gave the gum to him, he held her hand and said, "how about a date, baby?"

She recoiled; he followed, he blocked her path, held her waist and said, "don't be afraid of me, Baby. I ain't gonna hurt you. I been with white girls before."

At that point one of his friends came into the store and pulled him away. Caroline Bryant ran to the Milam's car which had a gun. When she returned, Till said, "bye, baby" and—later court testimony indicated—"wolf whistled" at her.

The encounter was enough. Was the "wolf whistle" Till's speech impairment from his childhood? No one in Mississippi would have known that—whatever the sound he may have made, it sounded like a sexual advancement to them. And he had grabbed her and, at least briefly, held her.

Emmett Till had done the unthinkable in Mississippi.

The wolf whistle was open to interpretation, even to those who knew him. A sixteen-year-old cousin, Maurice Wright said, "he had polio when he was three and he couldn't talk plain. You could hardly understand him." But two others, Wheeler Parker, from Chicago and Simeon Wright, both said that Till *had* whistled at the woman—Carolyn Bryant.

Roy Bryant returned from Texas on a Friday and learned of the encounter and questioned several black men who came to the store. Saturday was the busiest day at the store and he could do little then. He did not have an automobile, but he asked his half-brother, Milam, to meet him at 10:30 Saturday night, with Milam's '55 Chevrolet pick-up truck.

Stephen Whitfield writes:

> Milam was thirty-six years old, stood six feet two inches, and weighed 235 pounds. Like his half-brother, he was the father of two sons. A much-decorated combat veteran of the European Theater in World War II, he made a living by renting Negro-driven mechanical cotton pickers for plantations in the Delta. "Big" Milam was the sort of man who prided himself on getting along with blacks, on knowing how to "handle" them. He had a ninth grade education. Like Roy Bryant, Milam had a .45 Colt. Both men brought their automatic pistols to the home of "Preacher" Wright, which was

an unpainted cabin behind a cotton field off a gravel road nearby three miles east of Money. Both men were sober.

Bryant and Milam got to Wright's house between 2:00 and 3:30 a.m. Sunday August 28, 1955. There they questioned the residents and found which one was Till. They took him in the pickup and drove to the Clint Shurden Plantation in Drew, one of several locations where they stopped with Till. They pistol-whipped him at the planation and later in a toolshed behind Milam's house in Glendora.

Much later writer (and Mississippi native) William Bradford Huie interviewed Bryant and Milam. They told him that while they were beating Till, he called them bastards, declared he was as good as they (were) ... and in the past had sexual enccounters with white women. In an article by Huie in *Look* magazine, titled "The Shocking Story of Approved Killing in Mississippi," Huie quoted Milam:

> Well, what else could we do? He was hope-less. I'm no bully; I never hurt a nigger in my life. I like niggers—in their place—I know how to work 'em. But I just decided it was time a few pooplo got put on notice. As long as I live and can do anything about it, niggers are going to stay in their place. Niggers aren't gonna vote where I live. If they did, they'd control the gov-ernment. They ain't gonna go to school with my kids. And when a nigger gets close to a white woman, he'd tired o' livin'. I'd likely kill him. Me

and my folks fought for this country, and we
got some rights. I stood there in that shed and
listened to that nigger throw that poison at me,
and I just made up my mind. "Chicago boy," I
said, "I'm tired of 'em sending your kind down
here to stir up trouble. Goddam you—I'm going
to make an example of you—just so everybody
can know how me and my folks stand."

There are now differing accounts of where Till was
killed; either in the shed or along the Tallahatchie river.

Bryant and Milam then drove to a cotton gin and
took a 70 pound fan—worried then only because they
might be accused of stealing.

In *Death in the Delta*, Stephen Whitfield writes:

> They drove to a gin near Boyle, where Till
> was forced to lift a heavy fan into the truck. It
> was already daylight. They drove past Glendora,
> near where Milam hunted squirrels. Till was told
> to carry the fan to the riverbank, then to strip.
> He did not cry. Milam remembered taunting
> him in the basic vocabulary of white supremacy
> "Nigger, you still good as I am ?" Apparently the
> last words Emmett Till ever heard were Milam's
> second question: "You still done it to white girls
> and you gonna keep on doing' it ?" Then, accord-
> ing to their own account delivered after the
> trial, Milam fired one bullet at Till's head, joined
> Bryant in tying the fan to the victim's neck, and
> dumped the body into the Tallahatchie River.

After Bryant and Milam took Till away, Wright sat on his front porch for a while, then he and another man drove around Money trying to find Till. Curtis Jones then called the LeFlore County sheriff; Wright would not do so—he feared for his life if he did. Jones also called his mother in Chicago, who called Till's mother, Mamie Till Bradley; she called the Chicago police, who, in turn, began called sheriffs in Mississippi.

Soon the Mississippi field secretary for the National Association for the Advancement of Colored People, Medgar Evers and Amzie Moore entered the case ... even disguising themselves as cotton pickers and going to into the cotton fields in search of any information.

Less than three days later, Till's swollen and disfigured body was found by two boys fishing on the Tallahatchie river. It was an horrific discovery: his head had been badly damaged; he had been shot above the right ear; an eye was dislodged from the socket; there was evidence that he had been beaten on the back and the hips; his body was weighted to the fan blade which was fastened to his neck with barbed wire. He was nude, but wearing a ring with the initials "L.T." and the date "May 25, 1943" carved on it.

The ring was the clearest identification—the initials were those of Till's father. The body was, in fact, so mangled and decomposed that the ring was the *only* means of identification.

The beating, one policeman said, "was the worst he had seen in eight years of law enforcement."

The body was packed in lime and placed in a pine coffin. The body was not examined in Mississippi. Mamie

Till Bradley demanded that her son's body be brought back to Chicago for burial.

The events then in Chicago were just as horrific as the discovery of the body in the Tallahatchie in Mississippi:

> The A.A. Rayner Funeral Home in Chicago received Till's body, and upon arrival, (Mamie Till) Bradley insisted on viewing it to make a positive identification, later stating the stench from it was noticeable two blocks away. She decided to have an open casket funeral, saying, "There was no way I could describe what was in that box. No way. And I just wanted the world to see." Tens of thousands of people lined the street outside the mortuary to view Till's body, and days later thousands more attended his funeral at Roberts Temple Church of God in Christ. Photographs of his mutilated corpse circulated around the country, notably appearing in *Jet* magazine and *The Chicago Defender*, both black publications, and drew intense public reaction. According to *The Nation* and *Newsweek*, Chicago's black community was "aroused as it it has not been over any similar act in recent history." Till was buried September 6 in Burr Oak Cemetery in Alsip, Illinois.

Till's casket had a glass top.

At a press conference after the funeral, Mamie Till Bradley said, "Have you ever sent a loved son on vacation and had him returned in a pine box so horribly battered and waterlogged that someone needs to tell you that this sickening sight is your own son—lynched?"

In Mississippi, Bryant and Milam were indicted for murder. The trial was set to begin in September, 1955, in Sumner, Tallahatchie County.

Was the jury bi-racial?

In Mississippi? In 1955?

Jury members had to be voting citizens.

Stephen Whitfield writes:

> *... in Tallahatchie county ... none of the 19,000 Negroes were allowed to vote ...*

And, thus could not be on local juries.

Noted journalist David Halberstam called the trial "the first great media event of the civil rights movement."

And to call it a circus event is a vast understatement:

> Sheriff Strider welcomed black spectators coming back from lunch with a cheerful, "Hello niggers!" Some visitors from the North found the court to be run with surprisingly informality. Jury members were allowed to drink beer on duty and many white men in the audience wore handguns holstered to their belts.

The Prosecutor argued that Bryant and Milam kidnapped, tortured and killed Till and had thrown his body into the Tallahatchie river.

The defense argued that Bryant and Milam *had* taken Till, but let him go and, the body pulled from the

Tallahatchie river was too badly decomposed to be identified as Till's. Perhaps he had simply disappeared—back to Chicago, maybe, they hinted.

Bryant and Milam did not testify in court; they had a legal right not to testify, and surely their attorneys knew not put them on the stand.

The jury had three choices in the case: execution, life in prison or acquittal.

After arguments, the judge told the jury: take your time deliberating.

The jury came back in *67 minutes* with the verdict: Not Guilty. One jury member later said the jury would have reported sooner, but they were all drinking cokes in the jury room. Later, some jury members said they knew Bryant and Milam *were* guilty but felt execution or life in prison were too harsh; others said they believed the defense's case which said that prosecutors had not proven that Till had died or that it was his body in the Tallahatchie.

(Bryant and Milam could have also been indicted on kidnapping charges, but no one much bothered.)

Reaction nationally *and* internationally was immediate—and vitriolic.

In France, the newspaper *Le Figaro* stated "the scandalous verdict ... in acquitting Roy Bryant and John Milam ... when everything pointed to their shameful guilt, will arouse worldwide indignation." Which it did. The Vatican's *L'Osservatore Romano*, in a strong editorial against racism said that its American manifestations had "unfortunately, caused many crimes." In Düsseldorf, Germany, *Das Freie Volk* stated: "the life of a Negro in Mississippi is not worth a wolf whistle."

Only in Mississippi and other locales in the south, did newspapers agree with the verdict, including *The Memphis Commercial Appeal*, the *Greenwood Commonwealth* and the Greenville *Delta Democrat-Times*.

Journalist William Bradford Huie then later interviewed Bryant and Milam, in the offices of their lawyers, and later in a Holiday Inn. Bryant and Milam—and Carolyn Bryant—volunteered much; their lawyers asked some questions, because they themselves wanted to know the full truth. However the process was tainted—both Bryant and Milam were broke. Huie paid them between $3,600 and $4,000 for the interview. Paying for interviews—"checkbook journalism"—was largely considered unethical then and is considered even more so now. Huie, too, had reservations. "Other people find this sort of thing distasteful; I have not found it particularly pleasing," he said. But he acknowledged that paying the two was the only method of obtaining the truth.

Huie explained himself, with a typically backwoods phrase:

> "I am not a 'liberal'; I only write about the human race,(but)I don't try to reform it. I am capable of drinking out of the same jug with Milam and letting him drink first."

Bryant and Milam may have thought that the interviews with Huie would be hugely satisfying to their supporters and even cathartic to them, although with their rudimentary educations, neither would have probably understood the word *cathartic*, or ever used it.

And with the Not Guilty verdict, they were freed from the possibility of double jeopardy; being accused twice of the same crime.

They then admitted they killed Emmett Till.

The Huie article was published in *Look*, January 24, 1956 and was reprinted in the April 1956 issue of *Reader's Digest*. Huie also published the material in a paperback book, *Wolf Whistle* (1959), which had, he said, a one-million-copy first printing. Both the *Look* article and *Wolf Whistle* in retrospect, had factual or interpretative flaws, although Huie had the core of the case correctly stated. *Wolf Whistle* is now long out-of-print and even rare now among used- and rare-book dealers.

The Huie material reveals that neither Bryant nor Milam were ever ashamed of the kidnapping, torture and murder of Emmett Till. Nor did they express any remorse.

The aftermath of the Not Guilty verdict also included ...

... the Montgomery Bus Boycott begun by Rosa Parks and led by Parks and Martin Luther King began less than six months later.

... in 1991, a 7-mile stretch of 71st Street in Chicago was re-named the "Emmett Till Road."

... the "Emmett Till Memorial Highway" was dedicated between Greenwood and Tutwiler, Mississippi, the same route his body took enroute to Chicago. The road, however, intersects the H.C. "Clarence" Strider Memorial Highway. Strider was the sheriff who said "welcome niggers" at the Bryant-Milam trial.

... the James McCosh Elementary School, in Chicago, where Till had been a student in the seventh grade, was renamed the "Emmett Louis Till Math and Science Academy" in 2005.

... in 2007, Tallahatchie County issued a formal apology to Till's family. "We, the citizens of Tallahatchie County, recognize the Emmett Till case was a terrible miscarriage of justice. We state candidly and with deep regret the failure toeffectively pursue justice. We wish to say to the family of Emmett Till that we are profoundly sorry for what was done in this community to your loved one."

... also in 2007 Georgia Congressman John Lewis, whose skull was fractured while being beaten during the 1965 Selma march, sponsored a bill that provides a plan for investigating and prosecuting unsolved Civil Rights era murders. The Emmett Till Unsolved Civil Rights Crime Act was signed into law in 2008.

... and there have been memorials elsewhere.

Artists, writers and musicians have been haunted by the Emmett Till case. William Faulkner published two essays about the Till case and justice in Mississippi; Harper Lee published *To Kill a Mockingbird* in 1960, in which a white attorney defends a black man accused of raping a white woman. It is considered a classic of American literature and is still widely read. James Baldwin based his 1964 drama, *Blues for Mister Charlie*, loosely on the Till case. Bebe Moore Campbell's 1992 novel, *Your Blues Ain't Like Mine*, centers on the Till case. Toni Morrison's 1986 play was titled *Dreaming*

Emmett. Emmylou Harris included a song *My Name is Emmett Till* in her 2011 album *Hard Bargain*. Cornelius Eady published a poem, *Emmett Till's Glass-Top Casket*, Al Young wrote *The Emmett Till Blues*. And Bob Dylan wrote and has performed *The Death of Emmett Till*. The lyrics include:

> *I saw the morning papers but I could not*
>> *bear to see*
> *the smiling brothers walkin' down*
>> *the courthouse stairs.*
> *For the jury found them innocent*
>> *and the brothers they went free.*
> *While Emmett's body still floats the foam*
>> *of a Jim Crow southern sea.*

Till's body was exhumed and an autopsy conducted by the Cook County Coroner in Chicago, in 2005. Using DNA from Till's relatives, the body was positively identified as Till's. The autopsy showed extensive cranial damage, a broken left femur, and two broken wrists. Metal fragments found in the skull indicated he was shot with a .45 caliber gun. The body was reburied in a new casket. The original glass-topped casket is now at the Smithsonian.

The FBI re-opened the case in 2004. Their records and a transcript of the court proceedings are now available in book form, although much of it heavily redacted (omitted).

And what of Bryant and Milam? After the not guilty verdict and especially after publication of Huie's *Look* article, they quickly become pariahs. No one came to the Bryant store and no one hired Milam's work crews. Both became bankrupt. Both moved to Texas for several years then returned to Mississippi.

Milam died of cancer in 1980, at 64.

Bryant and his wife Carolyn were divorced. He remarried, operated a second store, in Ruleville, Mississippi and was convicted of food stamp fraud in 1984 and again in 1988.

In 1992, Bryant was interviewed about the murder, unaware that Till's mother was listening. He said that Till ruined his life, that he had no remorse and said, "Emmett Till is dead. I don't know why he can't stay dead."

Bryant died at 63, in 1994, also of cancer.

It is safe to say no one mourned their passing.

A 2009 picture of the Bryant grocery store, where Emmett Till encountered Carolyn Bryant, shows it abandoned and in ruins.

* * *

Willie Reed saw a pick-up truck going "real fast" near Drew, Mississippi, with four white men inside and three white men and a black man in the back. It parked near a barn as he entered a nearby store. He then heard "someone hollering" and sounds like someone was being beaten.

A month later, Willie Reed, then 18, testified in court that two of the men were Bryant and Milam. Reed had to walk a gauntlet of Klu Klux Klansmen to enter the courthouse.

Margalot Fox wrote in *The New York Times*, July 24, 2013:

Though the two white men tried for the murder were acquitted, the testimony of Mr. Reed was considered so powerful that it made him a hero of the movement—albeit a quiet, accidental and long unsung one, who spoke of the case only rarely and with obvious pain.

"Willie Reed stood up, and with incredible bravery pointed out the people who had taken and murdered Emmett Till," the filmmaker Stanley Nelson, who interviewed Mr. Louis for his 2003 documentary, "The Murder of Emmett Till," said Wednesday. "He was from Mississippi, and somewhere in his heart of hearts he had to know that these people would not be convicted. But he did what he had to do."

For decades, Mr. Louis told no one of his involvement in the case. Even his wife, Juliet, whom he married in 1976, did not learn of it until eight years later, when a relative told her.

He was spirited out of Mississippi right after the trial, for fear of deadly reprisals and settled in the Chicago area. He changed his last name from Reed to Louis and tried to cloak his life in anonymity. For years, his wife said, he had nightmares about the Till case.

Willie Louis, perhaps the last living link to the Till case, died July 18, 2013. He was 76. Had he lived, Emmett Till would have been 72.

Five |

1955: Rosa Parks

... the making of a Civil Rights icon ...

THE TURNING POINT OF the American Civil Rights movement may well have been December 1, 1955, in Montgomery, Alabama.

Rosa Parks was taking the Cleveland Avenue bus home that day, about six p.m. She paid the fare and moved to the Colored section in the back of the bus. Her seat was the first row directly behind the ten rows reserved for whites. When the bus filled up, with several white passengers standing, the driver James F. Blake, stopped the bus and moved the Colored sign *behind* Parks, expecting her, and three others, to obediently move farther back.

By her account, Blake said, "Y'all better make it light on yourselves and let me have those seats." He scarcely knew who he was talking to or what he had set in motion.

"Let me have those seats," he said.

"The other three moved but I didn't," she remembered. Instead, she moved to the window seat in the same row.

"Why don't you stand up?" the driver insisted.

"I felt determination cover my body like a quilt on a winter night," Parks later recalled.

"I don't think I should have to stand up."

"Well, if you don't stand up, I am going to have to call the police and have you arrested."

If anything, perhaps her determination deepened.

"You may do that," she said. And, she later recalled, "I would have to know for once and for all what rights I had as a human being and a citizen."

The "*you may do that*" in her response indicated an unspoken: *and then what will happen?*

It is something of a common myth among those who have little knowledge of that day and that brief confrontation, that she was simply too tired, her feet too sore, from a day at work, to move from her seat. Nothing could be further from the truth.

In her 1992 autobiography, *Rosa Parks: My Story* she wrote:

> People always say that I didn't give up my seat because I was tired, but that isn't true. I was not tired physically, nor no more tired than I usually was at the end of a working day. I was not old, although some people have an image of me as being old then. I was forty-two. No, the only tired I was, was tired of giving in.

And when she was arrested and taken away, she told the arresting officer, "Why do you push us around?" She remembered him saying, "I don't know, but the law's the law." She then later remembered thinking, "I only knew that, as I was being arrested, that was the very last time I would ever ride in humiliation of this kind."

It was *the very last time.*

And, in fact, she had been planning for that confrontation most of her adult life.

Her act began a 381-day boycott of the Montgomery transit system, led by a young and then-largely unknown Martin Luther King, Jr. (Participants used the word *protest*, as boycotts were illegal in Alabama.)

The Montgomery bus boycott is now considered the beginning of the American Civil Rights movement.

In a remarkable phrase, Eldridge Cleaver, author of *Soul on Ice*, said, "Somewhere in the universe, a gear in the machinery shifted."

So much so that, in the spring of 1989, when a single Chinese student stood defiantly in front of a line of Chinese Army battle tanks in Tiananmen Square, as hundred of millions of people watched around the world, it was, as South African president Nelson Mandela phrased it, "a Rosa Parks moment."

Rosa Parks—Rosa Louise McCauley—was born in Tuskegee, Alabama, February 4, 1913. No one now knows the location, but one photograph exists of her birthplace home:

> a plywood shanty fronted by six wobbly steps leading up to a porch seemingly on the verge of collapse, A portion of the front picture window has been shattered as though from a rock thrown into the living room, and the picket

fence that marks the property is severely splintered. But for a sturdy brick chimney, the edifice would appear no better than the sharecroppers' shacks photographed so hauntingly by Walker Evans in *Let Us Now Praise Famous Men*.

It could have, in fact, been identical to the shack where Emmett Till was kidnapped by Bryant and Milam, or something out of *The Grapes of Wrath*.

When she was two, she was baptized in the African Methodist Episcopal (AME) Church and, scarcely much older than that, began participating in church services which continued throughout her life. "There was a strange glow about Rosa—a kind of humming Christian light, which gave her a unique majesty," said James Farmer, founder of the Congress of Racial Equality (CORE).

About the same time, her mother moved to Pine Level, Alabama, a flyspeck on the map like Florida, Missouri, where Samuel Clemens was born. Parks' father, a carpenter and stonemason, built homes throughout the Black Belt area of Alabama. He left Pine Level to find work when she was a baby and she didn't see him again until she was five. Then he left again and she didn't see him until she was an adult and married.

Rose was usually alone and often ill—she suffered from chronic tonsillitis, and it was only when she was nine that her mother could afford to pay for a tonsillectomy.

And she not fully black, but was a mulatto. Her grandfather was so light-skinned and had such straight hair many thought him white. Her younger brother,

Sylvester, was so light-skinned that many thought him Asian and called him "Chink."

Her family moved to Montgomery in 1924, and, at 11, she was enrolled in the Montgomery Industrial School for Girls, established in 1866. It was a huge step from Pine Level, Alabama, to Montgomery. For the first time she saw, and lived in, a city.

Montgomery was fully Jim Crow, a phrase originally from a 1828 vaudeville song-and-dance act, "Jump Jim Crow," performed by white entertainer Thomas "Daddy" Rice, who appeared in black- face.

Douglas Brinkley writes:

> Beginning around 1875, black and whites were legally separated on streetcars, trains, steamboats, and every other mode of transportation, as well as at schools, hospitals, restaurants, hotels, barbershops, theaters and even drinking fountains. Segregation laws slapped "white" and "colored" signs on virtually every facility ...

Former Joint Chief of Staff Chairman and U.S. Army General Colin Powell once said, "the flame under the melting plot was unlit when it came to African Americans."

But the Industrial School for Girls, with an all-black student body, was forced to close; it had been a prime target of Montgomery segregationists. Rosa McCauley attended the ninth grade at Booker T. Washington Junior High School, and tenth and eleventh grade at the laboratory school at Alabama State Teachers College.

She wanted to be an educator (which, in fact, she was, during her civil rights activist years), but returned to Pine Level to care for her ill grandmother. When her grandmother subsequently died, Rosa returned to Montgomery, taking her first job, in a textile mill. She then had to quit that job to take care of her ailing mother.

Her life changed when she met and fell in love with Raymond Parks. He was a charter member of the Montgomery chapter of the NAACP. They were married in Pine Level in December, 1932.

He had been concerned about the Scottsboro Boys case, in which nine black boys were all accused of raping two white women, and he had set up a legal defense fund for the boys. Planning meetings about the case were then held in their front room. With some risk.

"There was a little table about the size of a card table," she remembered. "That table was covered with guns ....

> "I can remember sitting on the back porch with my feet on the top step and putting my head down on my knees, and I didn't move throughout the whole meeting. I just sat there. I guess there were about a half dozen men. I can't even remember who they were, although I probably knew them. After the meeting was over, I remember, my husband took me by the shoulders and kind of lifted me from the porch floor. I was very, very depressed about the fact that black men could not hold a meeting without fear of bodily injury or death."

While Parks continued his work with the NAACP, Rosa learned more and more. And perhaps became radicalized. He urged her to finish her high school education, which she did, in 1933. Raymond had quit the NAACP, but Rosa had joined.

She then got a job, working as a secretary—briefly—at Maxwell Field, an Air Base established by the Wright brothers. It was reasonably integrated, a remarkable difference from the rest of Montgomery. It showed her what the rest of society could—and should—be.

Her work in the NAACP and her attempts to vote opened her eyes. She tried to register to vote in 1943 by taking a test—and failed.

She had to take a bus to take the test a second time. The bus driver's name was James F. Blake. Parks boarded his bus through the front door; he told her she would have to get off and board though the back door. "I told him I was already on the bus and didn't see the need of getting off and getting back on when people were standing in the stepwell. He told me if I couldn't go through the backdoor that I would have to get off the bus—'my bus' he called it. I stood where I was."

She knew that one of his favorite tricks was to make "nigras" get out of the front door of the bus, and go to the back door. He would drive away before they could board through the rear door.

When he tugged her sleeve to push her off the bus, Parks did not struggle. She told him not to strike her—she would get off by herself. (She saw he carried a holstered pistol on his belt.) Then she dropped her purse and sat on a white only seat to get it. She had learned from Gandhi; *and* from the Bible but, as Martin

Luther King, Jr. once said, "eventually the cup of endurance runs over, and the human personality cries out, 'I can take it no longer.'"

Her confrontation with Blake in November, 1943 stayed with her; she never rode Blake's bus again—until December 1, 1955.

In April, 1945, she tried again to take the test to vote—for a third time—and this time passed.

She continued to work with the NAACP; she was not an organizer, rather a secretary, keeping the office functioning; but she also met all local and state NAACP officers and she did speak at NAACP meetings. She continued her work with the AME church. She was thrilled in May, 1954, when the Supreme Court ruled that separate public schools for whites and blacks was inherently unequal; thus the court reversed Plessy v. Ferguson, the 1896 Supreme Court case that essentially legitimized Jim Crow throughout the south.

On March 2, 1955 Claudette Colvin, then 15, boarded a Montgomery bus, which was empty. When the bus began to fill with white passengers, the driver ordered her and three others to move to the back. The three others did so; she refused. The police came, knocked her schoolbooks from her hands, handcuffed her despite her screams and arrested her for assault, disorderly conduct and violating the segregation laws.

It seemed a good time for a test case against the Montgomery transit system and the city of Montgomery. but then flaws appeared. At 15, Colvin was immature, did not present herself well, and, as was subsequently discovered, was several months pregnant. She was simply not the right person to be the focal point for a test case. Ultimately, she went to court, paid a small fine and returned to school.

Parks had attended the Highlander Folk School, a Tennessee Center which trained social activists, including Marion Barry Jr., Julian Bond, Martin Luther King, John Lewis and others. It was the completion of a perfect formula for her: her own deep faith and life-long participation in the AME church; her own native intelligence and sense of goodness; her local work with the NAACP and the Highlander training for workers' rights and social equality.

When Parks was confronted on the Montgomery bus December 1, 1955 by driver James Blake, who had mistreated her twelve years earlier, and who told her, "Well, I am going to have you arrested," she said, "you may do that."

The single word *may* placed her on a very high moral plane.

"When I made that decision, I knew I had the strength of my ancestors with me." And, as Douglas Brinkley writes, "And her formal dignified 'No,' uttered on a suppertime bus in the cradle of the Confederacy as darkness fell, ignited the collective 'no' of black history in American ...."

Her act was not exactly premeditated—perhaps not for that day at least—and she was not too tired from a day at work. But she knew of the burning injustices committed under the name of Jim Crow and of southern law. And she knew about, and became physically ill, when she saw the pictures of murdered Emmett Till, less than six months earlier. And so the time came.

Her arrest was processed at Montgomery's City Hall, and when she asked for a drink of water, she was refused by a white Montgomery policeman. "It's for whites only," he said. Then she thought of Roman soldiers who gave Jesus only vinegar on the road to Calvary.

She was booked into the city jail, fingerprints and mugshot taken, and she was placed in a single cell, only to be moved to a cell with two others. She was again refused a drink of water and only after an hour or so, was allowed to call home. She asked that her husband come get her.

Before he arrived the Montgomery black community knew all about her arrest.

Rosa?

They arrested our Rosa?

Sweet, kind, deeply spiritual Rosa Parks.

They arrested Rosa?

It was no small thing to decide to challenge the Jim Crow system. She risked her job, her family—she risked everything.

But by 11 pm. that same night, Rosa Parks decided to challenge the Montgomery bus system and the segregation laws in court, with the aid of the NAACP legal fund and whatever other help that could be offered.

She lost her job at her Montgomery Fair department store the next January, not exactly fired, they said, but because they were closing their tailor shop. (It was a blessing, she later said, as it relieved her of the burden of how to get to work without the Montgomery bus system.)

Jo Ann Robinson, head of the Woman's Political Council, which was made up of 300 of the area's most active integrationists, called friends. She was ready to distribute thousands of flyers urging a boycott of the Montgomery transit system. She was on the faculty of Alabama State University and used their mimeograph machines late at night to print flyers. It was she, perhaps more than Parks, who began the boycott. The flyers read:

> If we do not do something to stop these arrests, they will continue. The next time it may be you, or your daughter, or mother. This woman's case will come up on Monday. We are, therefore, asking every Negro to stay off the buses on Monday in protest of the arrest and trial. Don't ride the buses to work, to town, to school or anywhere on Monday.

In *Rosa Parks: A Life*, Douglas Brinkley writes that 3,500 of Montgomery's homes, schools and churches received the flyers.

In *The Autobiography of Medgar Evers*, Myrlie Evers-Williams and Manning Marrable state there were 35,000 flyers distributed.

Martin Luther King, Jr., pastor of the Dexter Avenue Baptist Church, was contacted and was, initially, reluctant to get involved, but soon agreed to join. He was 25 at the time.

The next Sunday's editions of the *Montgomery Advertiser* had a picture of the handbill on the front page, thereby insuring that thousands of readers who otherwise hadn't gotten a copy of the handbill now knew about it.

King said that if 60 percent of Montgomery's blacks participated in the boycott, it would be a success. The day after the article was published in the *Montgomery Advertiser*, when blacks should all be going to work, King looked out and saw that Montgomery buses—*all* were empty.

On December 5, she appeared in court for her trial. 500 black residents met her at the City Hall. Many remembered how dignified she was in a black dress, black hat and grey coat.

She was accompanied by the only two black lawyers in Montgomery, Fred Grey and Charles Langford. She pled not guilty, but the outcome was foregone. In five minutes she was found guilty, fined ten dollars and an additional four dollars in court costs.

On that same evening, Montgomery black leaders assembled at the Mt. Zion AME church, where local NAACP leader E.D. Nixon berated them for their lack of leadership in this crisis.

"You ministers have lived off these washwomen for the last one hundred years and ain't never done nothing for them. Little boys. We've worn aprons all our lives. It's time to take the aprons off .... If we're going to be men, now's the time to be men."

Martin Luther King, Jr. came late, just in time to hear those words.

"Brother Nixon, I'm not a coward. I don't want anyone to call me a coward."

"Somewhere in the universe, a gear in the machinery shifted," Eldridge Cleaver said, when Rosa Parks refused to give up her seat on the Montgomery bus.

Perhaps a second gear shifted that night; Martin Luther King, Jr. was elected leader of the Montgomery Improvement Association (MIA), the principal group leading the boycott. (Much to the dismay of E.D. Nixon, who thought then—and years later—that the leadership position should have been his.)

A rally was then held at the Holt Street Baptist Church; and traffic was snarled for blocks. Martin Luther King, Jr. spoke. About Rosa Parks:

> Since it had to happen, I'm happy it happened to a person like Rosa Parks. For nobody can doubt the boundless outreach of her integrity. Nobody can doubt the height of her character, nobody can doubt the depth of her Christian commitment. But there comes a time that people get tired. We are here this evening to say to those who mistreated us so long that we are tired—tired of being segregated and humiliated; tired of being kicked about by the brutal feet of oppression. We have no alternative but to protest. For many years we have shown amazing patience. We have sometimes given our white brothers the feeling that we liked the way we were being treated. But we come here tonight to be saved from the patience that makes us patient with anything less than freedom and justice.

At the end of the rally, the audience voted to support Rosa Parks in her legal fight *and* continue the bus boycott; it would continue unabated for another 13 months.

To the outside world, Rosa Parks was just a name; in the Montgomery black community, she became a twentieth-century saint. But—but—sainthood has its price. Her husband quit his job at the air base—the same base where she had worked, briefly—because, his boss said, no mention could be made of the bus boycott or her role in it. Her rent was raised and she began receiving death threats.

In December, Martin Luther King, Jr. and key members of the MIA presented reasonable demands to the bus system: hiring black drivers; courtesy to black passengers and seating on a first-come, first-served basis. The demands were refused.

In December, King began a boycott of all-white stores in Montgomery, just in time to cripple their Christmas season. Parks joined the boycott.

Martin Luther King, Jr. continued to lead the bus boycott, directing volunteers who used their own cars to transport workers wherever they need to go. The MIA eventually bought more than 15 station wagons to use as a private carpool system, years before that term became common. Each was registered by a local church with the church name painted on the sides; they were rolling churches and the occupants could occasionally be heard singing hymns inside.

Rosa Parks worked at a furious pace; coordinating car pools, and volunteering wherever she was needed throughout the Montgomery area. The work never seemed to end. Donations began to flow in from elsewhere, throughout the country, including shoes, for those who needed to walk to work. Parks matched the shoe sizes to those who needed them.

On January 26, Martin Luther King, Jr. was arrested for driving 30 miles an hour in a 25 mph zone. He was taken to jail, his mugshot taken, was fingerprinted and put in a jail cell. He was released before a riot could break out.

He soon got death threats, just like Rosa Parks had to endure:

> Nigger, we are tired of you and your mess now. And if you aren't out of town in three days, we're going to blow your brains out and blow up your house.

In his book, *Stride Toward Freedom*, King recalled, he heard an inner voice:

> Martin Luther, stand up for righteousness. Stand up for justice. Stand up for truth ... And lo, I will be with you even until the end of the world ... I heard the voice of Jesus saying still to fight on. He promised never to leave me, never to leave me alone. No, never alone.

Two days later, while he was speaking at a regular meeting of the MIA, a bomb exploded at his home. His wife and family were safe, but the bomb had blown out all front windows and left a hole in the concrete floor of the front porch. A crowd had gathered, becoming increasingly angry, but his calmness so reassured the crowd that it spontaneously began singing "Amazing Grace."

The bus boycott continued and white businesses were increasingly hurt by the lack of black customers. One day after the bomb exploded at King's house, a bomb was thrown at E. D. Nixon's house, the blast breaking windows in the neighborhood.

On February 2, 1956, Parks and 88 others were all indicted for violating an 1921 Alabama state statue barring boycotts.

Ultimately, Martin Luther King, Jr. was the only one of 89 actually tried. He was found guilty and had a choice: a $500 fine or 386 days in prison at hard labor. He lost an appeal and was forced to pay the fine in November, 1957. About that time, King became the key civil rights figure; Parks, secondary.

On August 25, a bomb was thrown at the home of Rev. Robert Graetz, which knocked out windows and caused other minor damage. Graetz was one of Parks' closest friends. The Montgomery mayor told reporters that he thought Graetz had thrown the bomb himself, for the publicity.

On November 13, 1956, the U.S. Supreme Court upheld the case of Browder v. Gayle, thereby invalidating all of Alabama's segregation laws. A headline in *The New York Times* read: "High Court Rules Bus Segregation Unconstitutional." Rosa Parks' name was not mentioned in the article; the omission was of little consequence to her.

Look magazine then came to Montgomery and asked to take photographs of her getting in, and off of, city buses. The photographer asked her to sit in a window seat and look out the window. The photograph became the world-wide iconic photograph of her. "It's become my symbol shot, my historical honor badge," she later said. Years and years later, she was still asked to sign copies.

She got on a Cleveland Avenue bus and was momentarily stunned to see driver James Blake. They ignored each other.

Segregationists did not give up easily:

A shotgun blast was fired at Martin Luther King, Jr.'s front door; Ralph Abernathy's parsonage was bombed; three other black churches were bombed and Rev. Graetz's home as bombed again, causing serious damage. Seven members of the Klu Klux Klan were arrested for the bombings and the Montgomery bus system ran normally.

But Parks continued to receive death threats; she finally knew it was time to leave Montgomery. Her younger brother Sylvester had moved north in 1946 and was working at a Chrysler plant. Rosa also moved to Detroit. She was there briefly, then got a job as a hostess at a guest residence supervising a small staff at the Hampton Institute, in Virginia. (It became Hampton University in 1984). While at Hampton she received a first copy of Martin Luther King, Jr.'s book, *Stride Toward Freedom*, his account of the Montgomery bus boycott.

She returned to Detroit for a Christmas vacation and decided to stay. She met Martin Luther King, Jr. again on June 23, 1963, when he spoke in Detroit, reminding his audience that segregation was still endemic in Michigan as well as in Alabama. One section of his speech included "I Have a Dream," a dress rehearsal for his August 23, 1963 Washington, D.C. speech when more than 250,000 people gathered at the Lincoln Memorial. It was the largest civil rights rally in U.S. history.

She had been working in a small clothing factory in Detroit, but the Washington rally re-energized her to return to activism; she began working on the Congressional campaign of a young John Conyers. Parks urged Martin Luther King, Jr. to come to Detroit and endorse Conyers, which he did. When Conyers won, he invited Parks joined his office staff. She worked for Congressman Conyers in his Detroit office from 1965 until she retired in 1988.

When she said *No* ... on the bus in Montgomery. *No. No more humiliation, no more segregation*, she started a boiling, rolling, tide of justice that had no stopping. One simple statistic tells the story:

> When Parks was arrested in 1955, Alabamans had not elected a single black official; in 1975 the state had 200 African-American office holders, including 13 of the 108 members of its lower house and 2 of its 36 state senators. Whereas fewer than 100 blacks held public office across the entire South on the bloody Sunday of March 1965, ten years later upwards of 1,700 did, and more than a million and a half Southern blacks had joined the voter rolls.

"Bloody Sunday" was the first Selma to Montgomery protest march:

> The first march took place on March 7, 1965—known as "Bloody Sunday"—when 600 marchers, protesting the death of Jimmie Lee Jackson and ongoing exclusion from the electoral process, were attacked by state and local police with billy clubs and tear gas. The second march was held the following Tuesday, and resulted in 2,500 protestors turning around after crossing the Edmund Pettus Bridge.
>
> The third march started March 16. The marchers averaged 10 miles a day along U.S. Route 80, known in Alabama as the "Jefferson Davis Highway." Protected by 2,000 National Guard under Federal Command, and many FBI agents and Federal Marshals, marchers arrived in Montgomery on March 24 and at the Alabama State Capital on March 25.
>
> The route is memorized as the Selma to Montgomery Voting Rights Trail and is a U.S. National Historic Trail.

The Selma-to-Montgomery marches helped pass the 1965 Voting Rights Act.

Additionally ... in the north in 1968, Shirley Chisholm had become the first black woman elected to the U.S. Congress, and across the country major cities had voted in African American mayors, including Coleman Young in Detroit, Tom Bradley in Los Angeles and Maynard Jackson in Atlanta.

How was her single 1955 act perceived by the nation? A simple chronology reveals:

1976   Detroit renamed 12th street "Rosa Parks Boulevard."

1979   The NAACP awarded her the Spingarn Medal, its highest honor.

1980   She received the Martin Luther King, Jr. Award.

1983   She was inducted into the Michigan Women's Hall of Fame for her achievements in Civil Rights.

1990   She was invited to be part of the group welcoming Nelson Mandela upon his release from prison in South Africa.

She was in attendance as part of Interstate Highway 475 outside Toledo, Ohio was named after her.

1992   She received the Peace Abbey Courage of Conscience Award along with Dr. Benjamin Spock and others at the John F. Kennedy Presidential Library in Boston. 1995 She received the Academy of Achievement's Golden Plate Award in Williamsburg, Va.

1996   She was awarded the Presidential Medal of Freedom, the highest honor given by the U.S. Executive branch of government.

1998   She was the first to receive the International Freedom Conductor Award given by the National Underground Railroad Freedom Center.

1999   She received the Congressional Gold Medal, the highest award given by the U.S. Legislative branch. The medal bears the inscription, "Mother of the Modern Civil Rights Movement."

She received the Detroit-Windsor International Freedom Festival Freedom Award.

Time magazine named her one of the 20 most influential and iconic figures of the 20th century.

President Bill Clinton honored her in his State of the Union Address. "She's sitting down with the first lady tonight and she may get up or not as she chooses."

2000   Her home state awarded her the Alabama Academy of Honor.

She received the first Governor's Medal of Honor for Extraordinary Courage.

By this time she had received two dozen honorary degrees from universities throughout the world.

She is made an honorary member of the Alpha Kappa Alpha sorority.

The Rosa Parks Library and Museum on the campus of Troy University in Alabama is dedicated to her.

2002   Scholar Molefi Asante included her on his list of 100 Greatest African Americans.

A portion of Interstate 10 in Los Angeles is named in her honor.

2003   Bus # 2857 on which Parks was riding in 1955 was restored and placed on display at the Henry Ford Museum in Michigan.

2004   The Imperial Highway/Wilmington station on the Los Angeles County Metro system was named the "Rosa Parks Station."

2005   Rosa Parks died October 24, in Detroit, of natural causes. She was 92.

Her coffin was flown to Montgomery and taken in a horse-drawn hearse to the St. Paul African Methodist Episcopal (AME) Church. A memorial service was held there. She was dressed in the uniform of an AME church deaconess. Condoleezza Rice, one of the speakers, said that if it hadn't been for Rosa Parks, she would probably not have become Secretary of State. From Montgomery her casket was transported to Washington, D.C. to lie in state in the Rotunda of the Capital. She was the first woman and the second black person to lie in state in the Capital. Her casket was then taken to Detroit. The funeral service was seven hours long.

On October 30, President George W. Bush issued a proclamation that all flags on U.S. public areas be lowered to half-staff on the day of her funeral.

Metro Transit in King County, Washington placed posters and stickers dedicating the first forward-facing seat in all its buses in her memory shortly after her death.

The American Public Transportation Association declared December 1, 2005, the 50th anniversary of her arrest to be a "National Transit Tribute to Rosa Parks Day."

On that anniversary, President George W. Bush signed Public Law 109-116 directing that a statue of Parks be placed in the United States Capitol's National Statuary Hall. In signing the resolution directing the Joint Commission on the Library to do so, he stated "By placing her statue in the heart of the nation's Capitol, we commemorate her work for a more perfect union, and we commit ourselves to continue to struggle for justice for every American."

A portion of Interstate 96 in Detroit was renamed the Rosa Parks Memorial Highway, in December.

2006 At Super Bowl XL, played in Detroit, long-time residents Rosa Parks and Coretta Scott King were remembered with a moment of silence.

In Nassau County, New York, the Hempstead Transit Center was renamed the Rosa Parks Hempstead Transit Center.

2007 Nashville renamed MetroCenter Boulevard the Rosa L. Parks Boulevard.

2009 The Rosa Parks Transit Center was opened in Detroit.

2010 A plaza in the heart of Grand Rapids, Michigan was named the Rosa Parks Circle.

2012   On a trip to Michigan, President Obama took a side-trip to the Henry Ford museum. He sat in Rosa Parks' seat in the original bus. An iconic photo, taken at the time, shows him looking out the window as she did, deep in thought.

A street in West Valley City, Utah is named Rosa Parks Drive.

2013   On February 1, President Barack Obama proclaimed February 4, 2013 as the "100th Anniversary of the Birth of Rosa Parks." He called upon all Americans to observe this day with appropriate service, community and education programs to honor Rosa Parks' enduring legacy."

On February 4, to honor her 100th birthday, the Henry Ford Museum declared the day a "National Day of Courage." The original bus was made available for all visitors to sit in the seat Rosa Parks refused to give up.

On February 4, birthday celebrations were held at the Davis Theater for the Performing Arts in Montgomery and at Troy University.

A U.S. postage stamp was issued in her honor.

On February 27, her likeness was unveiled in the National Statuary Hall, in Washington, D.C, following public law 109-116 signed by President George W. Bush that a statue of Parks be established at the National Statuary Hall.

Six |

1961: John Howard Griffin

*"If I returned home to my wife and children
they would not know me ...
I had tampered with the mystery of existence
and I had lost the sense of my own being."*

WHEN RAY SPRIGLE JOURNEYED into the segregated South to write the series "I was a Negro in the South for Thirty Days," he only *said* he was black. And he had a companion along, for safety.

John Howard Griffin made an astonishing journey— it very nearly cost him his soul, and could have cost him his life. *Black Like Me* has now been in print for over 50 years; it is a exceptionally compelling and moving book and his early history and what he left out makes his story even more astonishing.

Howard Griffin—he added John when he began writing because there was British poet named Howard

Griffin—grew up in Fort Worth, Texas. He could memorize a whole school course in one week, and given what the Fort Worth schools may have been like in the 1930s, he was supremely bored and dissatisfied. He saw an advertisement for a lycée, a French college-prep school and persuaded his parents to let him go to school. In France. By himself. At 15.

He was admitted to the Lycée Descartes in Tours, to study medieval Gregorian chants and, after graduation, obtained a scholarship to the University of Poitiers (at Tours). He took literature courses, but music and medicine were his passions. During his second year, he worked at the Asylum of Tours, as assistant to the Director, Dr. Pierre Fromenty.

But World War Two began and Fromenty was drafted into the French Army; Griffin was left in charge of the Asylum with its 120 patients. What he witnessed was the first of what he called *Encounters with the Other.*

> I worked in France smuggling Jewish people out of Germany until France fell. I was (then) twenty, a research assistant at the Asylum of Tours. When the war came, they conscripted all the doctors and medical students into the service. They couldn't conscript me because I was an American citizen. I was immediately ordered back to the U.S. I refused to go because France had formed me. How could I flee at this time of need?
>
> I was put in charge of the Asylum. Then I got involved with the French Underground, smuggling Jews out of Germany, across France,

into England, We would use Asylum ambulances, put the refugees in straitjackets and move them that way. They didn't have to speak. Many of them didn't speak French. They didn't have safe conduct papers, of course. We didn't know how to steal, we didn't know how to forge (documents). We were infants in this, but we did the best we could.

* * *

The Nazis were moving in. I will be haunted to my death by those scenes. We brought the people inside these rooms and kept them hidden. We had to tell the parents who had children under fifteen that we weren't going to make it. Suddenly I experienced a double reality. The first: a parent said, "It's all over for us. Take our children." We would move anybody under fifteen without papers. You sat there and realized these parents were giving their children away to strangers. The second: I could go downstairs and into the streets and find perfectly good men who went right on rationalizing racism ...

Before he was 21, Griffin was hunted by the Gestapo. He would have been shot on sight if found.

When a friend was shot, Griffin knew it was time to flee.

He was smuggled out of France, to England; he then returned to the United States.

"Having witnessed the tragic effects of the Holocaust, refined to hideous perfection by the Nazis, he never forgot the horror," Griffin biographer Robert Bonazzi has said.

In 1941, Griffin then enlisted in the Army Air Corps, at the time when the Army and Air Force were not yet separate. He was sent to the South Pacific, to the Solomon Islands chain, as a language expert. There he was to study the indigenous culture, translate the dialect of the native inhabitants and gain information on Japanese movements. He was able to chart the islanders' native language phonetically, for the first time. The language would place him in the Florida or Nggela Islands, just north of Guadalcanal. His phonetic translations of their language still exists, in Griffin archives.

He had seen how the Nazis institutionalized racism. In the South Pacific Griffin had another epiphany: at first he viewed the tribe as "primitives"—as *Other*. But when he could not navigate jungle paths without a five-year-old boy to guide him, it was clear that *he* was the inferior.

He spent one year on the remote island with the native tribe, then was assigned to the landing base at Morotai; Japanese plans a had been intercepted. Morotai could expect an invasion. Japanese forces were estimated at 47,000. Americans and Australian forces were about a tenth of that.

Griffin was near the landing strip one night when he heard the drone of the "Washing Machine Charlies," Japanese bombers overhead. He ran for a ditch for cover:

The black edge of a ravine we used for an ammunition dump brought me to a halt. I realized I had missed our bomb shelter by a hundred yards or more. I turned to go around the ravine, listening always to the planes and the pattern of explosions. Then I headed on at an exact angle.

If it dropped its bombs they would pulverize me. I heard the high startling screech and felt intestines convulse. For an instant, I stood paralyzed, listening to the bombs hurtle toward me. Without any voluntary movement of my own, I felt my body hurl itself over the cliff and crash into the ravine.

Two days later when I regained consciousness, I lay naked on a bed.

"I'm going back to my unit," he told the doctors.

"No, you're not," he was told. "You're going blind."

He had sustained a severe concussion; he suffered some permanent memory loss and vision damage.

Griffin had been in the Army for more than four years; in the Pacific for three years and three months. He was sent back to the states, to a mustering out center near San Francisco. Griffin passed all the final physical exams except for one: the vision test. He was told he had 20/200 vision.

I was stupefied. I felt I could see reasonably well and yet 20/200 meant that I could see at 20 feet what a person with normal vision would see at 200 feet. I was legally blind.

While being mustered out, Griffin saw brave black soldiers returning to savage racism and segregation in the United States.

Those who had sacrificed for their country, who won medals for bravery, were mustered out, only to become second-class citizens, some treated even worse than German prisoners of war held in the United States:

> We continued through a series of interminable lines. Standing in the sunlight, I saw a tall, heavily decorated black sergeant who was being berated by the young white corporal who had charge of getting our group into the proper lines.
>
> "You may be a damned hero overseas, but you're nothing but a nigger here—and don't you forget it."
>
> I approached the gathering group.
>
> The sergeant, his body in a violent tremble whispered: "I've been four years fighting for this mother-fucking country, I'll be damed if I am coming back to this shit."
>
> "You're coming back to it alright," the corporal shouted back.

The armed forces were not fully integrated until 1948 by President Harry Truman; the segregationist Jim Crow laws were not broken until the Supreme Court decision Brown v. Board of Education in 1954.

Griffin returned to Texas where the diagnosis of blindness was confirmed by a neurosurgeon. His eyesight had become so inadequate the neurosurgeon suggested that Griffin give up the idea of a career in medicine.

Griffin vowed to return to France and study. He journeyed to Fountainebleau in the summer of 1946 and began a deeply spiritual transformation:

> I feared myself—feared that I would not be able to cope with the temptation to play the tragic figure, to become the noble sufferer accepting the world's pity.
>
> I knew that my fiercest struggles would not be against losing sight, but against the assaults of public opinion about blindness that would judge my condition tragic.

Griffin first stayed in the Benedictine Convent of St. Jacques, in a world virtually unchanged since the middle ages. He began to get horrific headaches. He then moved to the Abbey of Saint Pierre of Solesmes, living like a monk. The Abbey was unheated and Griffin contacted malaria. He burned up with fever and fell unconscious, and could not survive long on the meager diet in the Abbey. He eventually moved to a villa nearby and trekked back and forth to the Abbey.

In the spring of 1947, John Howard Griffin was completely blind. A bright light directly over his head looked like a candle in a fog.

Every part of life posed a problem. How would be eat without spilling his food? How would he urinate without making a mess? He had met an old monk, also blind, who taught him how to use a commode without soiling himself. He learned to eat without spilling ....

Griffin returned home to Mansfield, Texas, 20 miles south of Fort Worth, where his parents had a farm.

He simply refused to be a victim.

He journeyed to Fort Worth, to the Lighthouse for the Blind, and "learned all the Brailles."

He raised stock and Toulouse geese and Golden Roller canaries. He fed and took care of his stock by feel. At the annual Southwestern Exposition and Fat Stock Show in Fort Worth, other ranchers said, "You don't need to feel sorry for him. He can do as good without his sight as the rest of us can with ours. He sure takes all the prizes."

None of the other ranchers would play poker with him if he used a deck of braille cards. They feared he could read the cards as they played; he couldn't do that, but he didn't tell them that.

In New Orleans he met Sadie Jacobs who had been blind since she was three; he learned to use a flexible white cane to navigate by himself. And he learned to conquer "the dumb look," the brutally severe phrase used to describe the blind who instinctively look upward and away from a speaker, as they talk. He looked at the speaker and animated his face as he talked.

He met critic John Mason Brown, who urged him to become a writer. "How can I do that?"

"Get paper and a typewriter and begin," Brown said, simply.

Griffin went back to the Lighthouse for the Blind and, in a weekend, learned to use a typewriter. His father helped convert a feed room in their barn into a studio. It was scarcely bigger than some rooms Griffin has stayed in, in the abbeys in France. And, he may have realized, to be used for the same purpose; study and meditation.

The characters and dialog began to flow; it was an epiphany for him. As with other countless other writers, the story took over .... Griffin titled his book *The Devil Rides Outside*, from an old French phrase "the devil rides outside the monastery"; i.e., the battle between the chaste world of the church and the profane outside world.

The Devil Rides Outside was published in the fall of 1952 by a Texas publishing firm, Smiths, Inc.

It became a Book of the Month club selection. His first book. Written while he was blind.

His secret was out. At least in Texas. Newspaper headlines in Texas told the story:

Blind War Veteran's Book
To be Sent to 300 Reviewers

Blind Man Writes Way Into Catholic Church

Blind Man's Book Draw Praise From
Nation's Literary Critics

Blind Author Off to Consult Literary Critics

Success for Blind Author

Novel Written in Barn at
Mansfield Praised Highly

Only those outside Texas who read the first hard-cover copy with a dust jacket understood what an achievement that was for Griffin. On the back of the dust jacket Griffin is pictured outside, sitting on a large rock bench, with black glasses and holding a white cane. Obviously blind.

He eventually told Studs Turkel:

> I learned to type and wrote six books. They'd say "You're extraordinary." I'd say I'm not. It's just that I refuse to let them put me into a cloistered workshop. I resent very deeply the underchallenging of the blind, the young, the black.

A paperback version of the book was published by Pocket Books in 1954. It was banned in Detroit and became a test case. Eventually the U.S. Supreme Court ruled it was not obscene, a victory for all writers, publishers, readers and libraries.

He subsequently wrote *Nuni*, meaning world, in 1956, a novel based on the South Pacific tribe he had lived with, for a year.

The Devil Rides Outside is an anachronism, more Voltaire, perhaps than twentieth-century European; *Nuni*, a curiosity.

Griffin met Elizabeth Ann Holland, and despite his reservations, they were married, June 2, 1953. Griffin said:

> I had always been considered controversial,
> yet I felt not controversial at all. I was sightless
> but refused to live down to the sighted view that
> I was handicapped. I was a writer who refused
> to spin out popular books. If I allowed myself to
> became average—a totally dependent blind man
> or an unscrupulous writer—I could never be
> normal or live naturally. That was not bravery
> on my part, but simply survival.

On January 9, 1957 a remarkable thing happened. *A most remarkable thing.*

John Howard Griffin's eyesight came back.

He was outside, walking toward the back door—he didn't hit his head or suffer any accident, but his eyesight suddenly came back.

> Redness swirled in front of my eyes. I
> thought I saw the back door, cut in portions
> dancing at crazy angles ...

He called his wife who called their doctor. The sudden return of his eyesight, rudimentary as it was at first, threw him into a near nervous breakdown. He could see vague colors, blurring, then other colors and blurs. The doctor gave him a shot of demerol, a slight sedative. His parents arrived. All was chaos; Griffin in a near panic.

He saw his wife and his two children—for the first time.

Texas newspapers loved the story even more than the previous "Blind Author Writes Book" headlines:

"Suddenly I Could See":
Novelist Regains
Long Lost Vision

Finally Sees Children
Blind Author Regains
Sight After 10 Years

Author Still Glorying
In Restoration of Sight

His Sight's Restored,
He's Still Dumfounded

Griffin in Seclusion
To Avoid Pressures

To avoid reporters and additional turmoil, Griffin retreated to a nearby Carmelite monastery; he always felt safest, and with more peace of mind, in a cloistered environment.

He was given special glasses to help focus the muscles of his eyes; it took several weeks for his eyes to readjust and ever afterward he wore special glasses to protect his eyes.

What was the cause of his blindness and why did his eyesight return after 10 years, so unexpectedly and suddenly?

The best guess about his blindness was a severe concussion in the Japanese bombing and undiagnosed diabetes. Why his eyesight suddenly came back *ten years later*, is still a mystery.

His eyesight fully recovered, his first project was a "work for hire"—the First National Bank of Midland wanted a book to commemorate a new bank building. Griffin was paid $10,000 to write the book. He sorely needed the money. He worked and overachieved—his first draft was 1,300 pages. The final book, as printed, was 180 pages. Published in 1959, and titled *The Land of the High Sky*, Griffin described the history, the geography, the geology, the growth and the culture of the high plains. It had no distribution except as give-away copies for the bank. As rare as it is now, it is still a readable chronology of that area.

His eyesight restored, one would think that Griffin would simply want to enjoy his wife and children and lead a normal life.

And yet ... and yet ...

He told his wife ...

I have something I need to do ... I need to become black to know what's like to be black ...

She may have said, *you want to do what?!?* But her public response was "if that's what you have to do, that's what you have to do."

Griffin journeyed to New Orleans, where he had earlier learned to use a flexible white cane and picked a dermatologist out of the telephone book. He said, "I need to become black." The dermatologist said, "We can do that, but it'll take weeks."

"Not weeks," Griffin said. "One week."

Robert Bonazzi later quoted Griffin and explained:

"I could have been a Jew in Germany, a Mexican in a number of states or a member of any 'inferior' group. Only the details would have been different. The story would be the same." *Black Like Me* is, of course, the historical record of what it was like to be a Negro in the Deep South prior to the civil-rights era of the 1960s. It is also an intensively lived experience, evoked by the immediacy of his vital, vivid pose, that has kept open a window on that historical time.

One week. He wanted to become black in one week. Griffin lived in a guesthouse, on the New Orleans property owned by friends, Harold and Gladys Levy. Griffin took medicine and lay under sunlamps for 15 hours day. The medicine was Oxsoralen, which could potentially cause liver damage; the minor side effects were nausea and fatigue. The guesthouse was originally a slave cabin. Becoming black while living in a former slave cabin was an irony not lost on Griffin. He did not mention Harold or Gladys Levy by name in *Black Like Me* for fear of reprisals.

He saw the dermatologist for the last time November 7, 1959. The doctor suggested that he shave his head, as his hair would be a tipoff that he wasn't black. "Now you go into oblivion," the doctor said.

Alone, in the slave cabin, he shaved his head in the dark—as he had learned to shave while he was blind, it wasn't a problem. He applied coat after coat of stain, washing off the excess, applying more. He finally turned on a light standing in front of a mirror:

I stood in the darkness before the mirror, my hand on the light switch. I forced myself to flick it on.

In the flood of light against white tile, the face and shoulders of a stranger—a fierce, bald, very dark Negro—glared at me from the glass. He in no way resembled me.

The transformation was total and shocking. I had expected to see myself disguised, but this was something else. I was imprisoned in the flesh of an utter stranger, an unsympathetic one with whom I felt no kinship. All traces of John Howard Griffin I had been were wiped from existence. Even the senses underwent a change so profound it filled me with distress. I looked into a mirror and saw nothing of the white John Howard Griffin's past. No, the reflections led back to Africa, back to the shanty and the ghetto, back to the fruitless struggles against the mark of blackness. Suddenly, almost with no mental preparation, no advance hint, it became clear and permeated my whole being. My inclination was to fight against it. I had gone too far. I knew now the there is no such thing as a disguised white man, when the black won't rub off. The black man is wholly a Negro, regardless of what he may have been. I was a newly created Negro who must go out that door and live in a world unfamiliar to me.

The completeness of this transformation appalled me. It was unlike anything I had ever imagined. I became two men, the observing one and the one who panicked, who felt Negroid even unto the depths of his entrails. I felt the beginnings of a great loneliness, not because I was a Negro, but because the man I had been, the self I knew, was hidden in the flesh of another. If I returned home to my wife and children they would not know me. They would open the door and stare blankly at me. My children would want to know who is this large, bald Negro. If I walked up to friends, I knew I could see no flicker of recognition in their eyes.

I had tampered with the mystery of existence and I had lost the sense of my own being. That is what devastated me. The Griffin that was had become invisible.

In a remarkable phrase, Robert Bozanni said that Griffin became black "through a crude but mysterious alchemy," the consequences of which Griffin could only barely imagine.

The word in German is *doppelgänger*, a ghostly second self, but there is no reference to this sort of second self.

In *Man in the Mirror*, Robert Bonazzi writes:

> This seminal passage from *Black Like Me* reads like "a shock of recognition" scene in a modern literary novel. but there is a curious inversion for, in fact, the passage is most notable for its lack of recognition. Within that illuminated exposure, Griffin's entire psyche was overwhelmed by a series of nearly simultaneous

disruptions. His involuntary reaction to that sudden crisis was massive denial.

* * *

Unconsciously, Griffin had projected a primordial shadow figure, causing him to recoil from the truth. The repressed prejudices he had managed for so long to deny or rationalize were exposed with brutal clarity in the "stranger's" glare. The shadow figure was none other than the *Other*—the beast from the jungle of his deepest shame. Without warning, Griffin encountered his own racism face to face.

Griffin went out into the world and instantly had to learn how to be black in the south. He took a bus—buses in New Orleans were integrated by then—and sat in the middle and when a white woman entered, got up to give her his seat. Then realized that isn't done: it indicated surrender on the part of blacks. Then he tried to make eye contact with her. That wasn't done either. Then he heard it: *nigger*. It was aimed at him.

Before he became black, he had his shoes shined at a sidewalk shoeshine stand. After he made the transformation, he again returned to the shoeshine stand. The shoeshine man, Sterling Williams, was black.

"Ever seen these shoes before?" Griffin asked him.

"Seems like I'd seen a pair like them on a white man last week."

Griffin convinced Williams that he had been that white man—Williams was dumbfounded at the idea. Griffin very much needed a mentor; Williams helped show him *how to be black*. The episode with Griffin and Williams is the only wry part of *Black Like Me*.

Griffin initially wanted his book to be a dry sociological study, but with his not-fully-understood change, his raw emotions and his experiences, it became a first-person narrative, a diary/litany of his emotions and reactions.

Written more than 50 years ago, his voice speaks as powerfully now as it did then:

October 28, 1959

I was prepared to walk into a life that appeared suddenly to be mysterious and frightening.

October 29:

I felt the beginning loneliness, the terrible dread of what I decided to do.

November 7:

The transformation was total and shocking. I had expected to see myself disguised, but this was something else. I was imprisoned in the flesh of utter stranger, an unsympathetic one with whom I felt no kinship. All traces of the John Howard Griffin I had been were wiped from existence. Even the senses underwent a change so profound it filled me with distress.

November 8:

My flesh prickled with shame ...

November 10-12:

I left, sick with exhaustion, wondering where a Negro could sit to rest.

November 14:

I knew I was receiving what the Negroes call "the hate stare." It was my first experience with it. It is far more than look of disapproval one occasionally gets. This was so exaggerating hateful ...

He traveled from New Orleans into Mississippi and from there into Alabama. Between Mobile and Montgomery he got a ride from a white man in a a truck:

"Where you from?"

"Texas."

"What're you doing down here?"

"Just traveling around, trying to find jobs."

"You're not here to stir up trouble, are you?"

"Oh God, no."

"You start stirring up these niggers and we sure as hell know how to take care of you."

"I don't intend to."

"Do you know what we do to troublemakers down here?"

"No, sir."

"We either ship them off to the pen or kill them."

Griffin told the rest of the story, as if it had been seared into his memory, which it surely had:

He spoke in a tone that sickened me, casual, merciless. I looked at him. His decent eyes turned yellow.

I knew that nothing could touch him to have mercy once he decided Negroes should be "taught a lesson." The immensity of it terrified me. But it caught him up like a lust now. He entertained it, his voice unctuous with pleasure and cruelty. The highway stretched deserted through the swamp forests. He nodded toward the solid wall of brush flying past our windows.

"You can kill a nigger and toss him into the swamp and no one will ever know what happened to him."

They were virtually the same words Bryant and Milam may have said to Emmett Till before they killed him.

Griffin's odyssey took him from New Orleans through Mississippi and Alabama toward Atlanta. By accident, he made a horrific mistake by changing back and forth too quickly:

I developed a technique of zigzagging back and forth. In my bag I kept a damp sponge, dye, cleansing cream and Kleenex. It was hazardous, but it was the only way to traverse an area both as Negro and white. As I traveled, I would find an isolated spot, perhaps an alley at night, or the brush beside a highway, and quickly apply the dye to face, hands and legs, then rub off and reapply until it was firmly anchored in my pores. I would go through the area as a Negro, and then, usually at night, remove the dyes with cleaning cream and tissues and pass through the same area as a white man.

But that technique was too exhausting: he nearly lost his soul; the gyroscope of his being had spun out of control.

When he got to Atlanta, he cleaned off the dye in a bus station restroom and returned to Texas.

Prior to his trek through the South, he had arranged with *Sepia* magazine, in Fort Worth, a large-sized national magazine for black readers, patterned on *Life*, *Look* and *Colliers*, to run segments of his trip in a series. The first article was set for publication in the March 17, 1960, issue, but was bumped back to the April 17 issue.

Before the first article appeared, Griffin was receiving death threats by mail and on the telephone from racists in his own hometown of Mansfield, Texas.

He began keeping a shotgun near the front door.

Then he received a telephone call from the *Fort Worth Star-Telegram*. Did he know what had happened? A dummy had been hanged from the only stoplight in Mansfield. It was half white and half black with a yellow stripe down its back.

"It wasn't a very good likeness," Griffin said.

Griffin had fled the Gestapo in France; had been bombed by the Japanese in the South Pacific and now he was forced to flee his own hometown. He and his family and parents moved to Morelia, Mexico, 130 miles west of Mexico City, where his brother had some property. Griffin worked on *Black Like Me* there, for nearly a year. Then they were forced to flee *again*, by a regional uprising of Mexican Communists.

Black Like Me was published in hardcover in August, 1961, by Houghton Mifflin; it eventually sold 100,000 copies. There were exceptional reviews in *Booklist* magazine, *The Christian Century*, *Commonweal*, *Kirkus*

Reviews, Library Journal, The New York Herald Tribune, The San Francisco Chronicle, The Saturday Review of Literature, The London Times and others. Malcolm X mentioned it in his *Autobiography of Malcolm X.*

The publication created a firestorm for Griffin. He spoke and lectured and appeared nationally for a decade. He was not surprised when the book was totally ignored by publications in the south, except in Hattiesburg, Mississippi where the local newspaper publisher was a friend of Griffin's.

He had earlier been warned not to travel alone in the south. But almost 15 years later, in 1975, *almost 15 years* after the publication of *Black Like Me*, when he assumed all the controversy was over, he returned to Mississippi, alone. The Klu Klux Klan had never forgotten; they found him one night and nearly beat him to death with chains. He sustained permanent kidney damage but never mentioned the incident in his writings or speeches: he kept on speaking about racial justice; he could not do otherwise.

Griffin was always a devout Catholic, a Third Order Carmelite, a married man who could conduct services. He was also a great admirer (and personally, very similar to) Catholic monk Thomas Merton, who published over 70 books, who died December 10, 1968, at 53. Griffin was eventually chosen to write the authorized biography of Merton. Griffin traveled back and forth from Texas to the Abbey of Gethsemani, in Kentucky, and lived in the sparse cabin where Merton had lived as a hermit/monk. Griffin published books about the Catholic church and published books about Merton, but never completed the major biography he had planned.

Griffin appeared to be robust, but suffered serious illness throughout his adult life: malaria in France; then the decade of blindness; then foot tumors; spinal malaria which kept him paralyzed for a year; diabetes, which was perhaps the cause of his blindness. Diabetes led to osteomyelitis, an inflammation of the bone narrow of the lower spine.

Permanent kidney damage by the Klu Klux Klan. Loss of a part of one jaw, eventually a part of one leg, lung congestion, high blood pressure. Heart disease. A series of heart attacks. (At one point, at home in Texas, he had a heart attack, while no one else was in the house. He fell to the floor; when he was able to stagger to his feet, he had a second heart attack.)

And, while living in Merton's cabin, he was once struck by lightning.

He suffered all these with the stoicism of a twentieth-century Job.

The Oxsoralen to dye his skin black apparently did no damage, nor did his habit of heavy smoking.

John Howard Griffin died September 9, 1980 of a cerebral hemorrhage. He was barely 60. Shortly after his death, his wife was asked what he died of. "He died of everything," she said.

The Devil Rides Outside, *Nuni* and many of his other books are forgotten now, but *Black Like Me* is his true legacy to the world. It has been published in 65 countries throughout the world and has been in print for over 50 years. The chronology of *Black Like Me*:

1961   Hardcover edition published by Houghton Mifflin.

1962   Paperback edition published by Signet.

Canadian hardcover edition.

British hardcover edition.

French edition, paperback.

Polish edition, paperback.

1963 Dutch edition, hardcover.

Italian edition, paperback.

Portuguese edition, paperback.

1964   Norwegian edition, hardcover.

1965   British paperback edition.

Dutch paperback edition.

1966   Hungarian edition, paperback.

1967   Japanese hardcover edition.

Japanese paperback edition.

Braille edition.

Boxed set with *The Roses of Dallas*, about the JFK assassination.

1968   Danish edition, paperback.

Swedish edition, paperback.

Norwegian edition, paperback.

1976   Czechoslovakian edition, paperback.

Black Like Me second U.S. edition.

1977   Second Signet paperback edition.

1987   Second edition, Signet Paperback library, NAL/Penguin.

1996   35th anniversary edition, Signet.

2001   Limited Edition, hardcover.

2003   U.S. trade paperback edition, New American Library.

2004   Audio book and CD.

        Griffin Estate edition.

2006   Revised Griffin Estate edition.

        Japanese translation.

2009   German edition in English.

2009   United Kingdom edition.

2011   50th anniversary year of publication.

Black Like Me continues to be read. According to Robert Bonazzi, literary executor of the Griffin estate, as of July, 2013, the United Kingdom edition is available in 172 countries throughout the world; it is in print in France, South Korea, and Japan. Russia and China have printed pirated editions for years. In the United States, the Penguin paperback edition sells 50,000 copies a year; hardcover and e-book editions sell another 20,000 copies or more, not an insignificant amount after 50 years. It was once available in *every* European language.

Seven |

1963: Medgar Evers

Murdered in Jackson, Mississippi, June 12, 1963
Age: 37

WHEN JOHN HOWARD GRIFFIN was mustered out of the Army Air Corps, at an armed forces facility near San Francisco, he met racism, virtually face to face. He wrote about it in *Black Like Me.*

It bears repeating, in another context:

> We continued through a series of interminable lines. Standing in the sunlight, I saw a tall heavily decorated black sergeant who was being berated by the young white corporal who had charge of getting our group into proper lines.
>
> "You may be a damned hero overseas, but you're nothing but a nigger here—and don't you forget it."
>
> I approached the gathering group.

The sergeant, his body in a violent tremble whispered

"I've been four years fighting for this mother-fucking country, I'll be damned if I am coming back to this shit."

"You're coming back to it alright," the corporal shouted back.

Medgar Evers served in the Army in Europe in World War Two, including the battle of Normandy. Like the un-named sergeant in Griffin's anecdote, Evers was also a sergeant and was honorably discharged.

The same racial confrontation could have also happened to him.

Medgar Evers was born in Decatur, Mississippi, July 2, 1925; he walked twelve miles to school to earn his high school diploma. From 1943 to 1945 he was in the Army and upon returning, he knew he had to have more education. He applied to Alcorn College, a historically black college, now Alcorn State University. He was a football star, on the track team and debating team, sang in the choir and was a member of the business club. He edited the student newspaper and worked with the YMCA. He was listed in *Who's who Among Students in American Colleges and Universities* and was editor of the 1951 Alcorn student yearbook.

He met Myrlie Beasley on her first afternoon at Alcorn. He was older, had been in the service and was an achiever at Alcorn. They quickly became engaged.

Medgar and Myrlie were married Christmas Eve, 1951.

Medgar graduated from Alcorn and began working for Dr. Theodore Roosevelt Mason ("T.R.M.") Howard, of Mount Bayou, Mississippi, selling insurance for the Magnolia Mutual Life Insurance Company. There was virtually nothing in Mount Bayou, including no television; Myrlie saw everything that was missing in their lives there, but Medgar didn't seem to care. She worked as a secretary in the same office.

And he soon joined the NAACP.

It was a whole new education for Medgar Evers, journeying into the flat, stark Delta of Mississippi. He began setting up clandestine meetings, on behalf of the NAACP. Sharecroppers there couldn't read and knew little of their own culture; and almost nothing about historical figures in black history.

He educated them with the most simplistic techniques. He would take a commemorative George Washington Carver coin out of his pocket. "This is a colored man," he told them. And then he talked about Marcus Garvey, Harriet Tubman, Frederick Douglass and Marian Anderson, names they knew nothing about.

And he helped try and find Emmett Till.

He also listened to a speech by E.J. Stringer, who was the president of the Mississippi chapter of the NAACP. He, like Evers, had graduated from Alcorn, but he had to go out of state to get a degree in dentistry. "Is there anyone who would help integrate the state universities in Mississippi?"

Evers said he would. He then applied for admission to the University of Mississippi Law School. The NAACP Legal Defense Fund director-counsel, Thurgood Marshall, would be his attorney.

Myrlie Evers was terrified at the potential consequences; she knew there might be threats on their lives—or worse.

The University of Mississippi tuned down his application, as everyone expected. But in an accident of timing, immediately after their ruling, the U.S. Supreme Court announced the verdict in Brown v. Board of Education, that stated separate school systems for blacks and whites were essentially unequal. Segregation came down throughout the United States. Most southern states were at least nominally resigned to the decision: Mississippi was not.

In June, 1954 Judge Thomas Brady spoke in Greenwood, Mississippi. He had studied at Yale and Ole Miss. But he was an ardent segregationist. He was so pleased with his lecture he subsequently published it booklet form, *Black Monday*, about the Supreme Court decision.

In the audience was Bryon De La Beckwith, a runty child-man with a fractured family background. He had dropped out of college in the middle of his first semester, subsequently joined the Marines, and just barely met the physical requirements. He was in the Battle of Tarawa, in the Pacific, was wounded and sent home. He was a hater; he had a hatred, a bitterness about most everything but was not articulate enough to explain what he hated or why. But he did agree with everything Judge Brady said about segregation.

Beckwith subsequently married one Mary Louise Williams, a Wave he met while he was in the service. He was an uneducated, nasty, unrepentant racist; she was unladylike (her nickname was Willie), profane, unattractive and a heavy drinker. He apparently worshipped her. They were married, fought and divorced, then remarried, fought and divorced again. Then remarried again, for a third time. They gave a whole new meaning to the phrase "a marriage made in heaven."

Another Mississippian, Robert Patterson, and others, formed the (white) Citizens' Council. Beckwith joined. Much later, Beckwith was accused of being a member of the Klu Klux Klan. He denied it.

Medgar Evers accepted the job as the first Mississippi Field Secretary for the NAACP, November 27, 1954. The national NAACP leadership had a simple plan: change the laws and then change society.

He had to leave his insurance job, which was financially worrisome for them, but at least leaving Mount Bayou to relocate to Jackson, the state capital, was a positive move, Myrlie Evers thought.

As Mississippi Field Secretary, Evers sent monthly reports, memoranda and speeches to the national NAACP offices.

In 2005, long after his murder, his widow, then Myrlie Evers-Williams, and Manning Marable edited his documents and published *The Autobiography of Medgar Evers*. It is not a true autobiography nor a biography: the sub-title explains the format; *A Hero's Life and Legacy Revealed through His Writings, Letters and Speeches*. (The book also contains eight documents after he was murdered in June, 1963.)

His first report from Mississippi is typical of those he sent on to the NAACP national office. In this report, he does not refer to himself, as the applicant to the University of Mississippi Law School (in the second paragraph):

December 1954

Report on Mississippi

In 1954 there were a number of things that happened in Mississippi that we deem progress, and of course the unequaled leadership that the National Association for the Advancement of Colored People provided was unquestionably the reason for such. Certainly other organizations had their effects, particularly the Regional Council of Negro Leadership, but the unwavering position taken by the NAACP was phenomenal in Mississippi.

For the first time in the history of the University of Mississippi a Negro made a formal application to its School of Law. There had been no other formal application by a Negro to any "white" school in the state of Mississippi since Reconstruction.

The NAACP here was instrumental in getting the application for Ole Miss. Even though the applicant was not admitted his application is still pending for further consideration.

The governor of Mississippi ... was told that 99 percent of the Negro population of Mississippi, which is 45 percent of the total 2,200,000, was in favor of voluntary continued segregation. Now, this happened after the historic decision of the U.S. Supreme Court of May 17, 1954.

Now to prove his theory, the governor decided to call in a cross-section of Mississippi Negro leadership for July 30,1954, which naturally had to include the "radical" NAACP head,

Dr. E.J. Stringer, whom the governor would have been most pleased not to have invited, since he had already called in his "good" Negro leaders and briefed them on just what he wanted from them. However, since Dr. Stringer was also endowed by God to use his thinking facilities in the case of emergencies, he immediately called for a statewide meeting of Negro leadership including the governor's good Negro leaders. Now the governor, with his groundwork laid, was caught in a rather precarious position when more than two hundred (200) Negroes, representing many civic, religious, and fraternal organizations turned out just five days prior to his meeting which had been scheduled for the same issue for discussion, but from a different point of view.

And on that momentous day July 30, 1954, ninety-nine (99) out of one hundred (100) Negro leaders before the governor of Mississippi and his Legal Educational Advisory Committee, of which the governor is chairman, told him in no uncertain terms that they would have no part in any scheme to circumvent the U.S. Supreme Court's decision on segregation in the public schools, thereby immediately putting a public end to the propaganda that 99 percent of the Negroes in Mississippi favored continued segregation.

As a result of the governor's tremendous defeat here, he immediately retreated to an abolition plan which he had previously opposed most vigorously. The LEAC (Legal Educational Advisory Commission) drafted plans to abolish the public school which gives and was given (by votes 2-1) by the Mississippi legislature the authority to abolish the public schools to preserve segregation.

Citizens' Council Rise

Now during this time, "grass roots" vigilante groups began to form which called themselves "Citizens' Councils" but more appropriately called by Hodding Carter, Editor and Publisher of the Delta Democrat Times, Greenville, Mississippi, as the "uptown" Klu Klux Klan because so many of the towns being members and holding key official positions. Possibly four (4) out of five (5) bank officials, presidents or vice, hold a key position in the Councils. Particularly is this true in the Delta counties where in some counties Negroes outnumber whites as much as 3-1 in population. Bolivar County is an example: there are 19,000 whites and 46,000 Negroes, and of course Bolivar County has one of the strongest Councils in the Delta.

Objective: "Keeping the Negro in his place."

1). Keep him out of white schools.

2). Keep the ballot out of his reach.

3). Keep him dependent.

Evers then has a paragraph devoted to each of the numbered topics.

Tensions grew and grew in Mississippi; the state spiraled downwards toward terror and anarchy. There were death lists printed in public in newspapers in the state. The name of Medgar Evers was on them. Evers— and many others—knew what J. Edgar Hoover thought of the Mississippi chapter of the NAACP: Hoover believed it was a communist front organization. Evers knew he and the NAACP could get no help from Hoover.

Evers became guarded; his wife and children were taught to duck down, inside the house, if they heard a shot.

On the evening of June 12, 1963, just hours after President John F. Kennedy's nationally-televised speech on civil rights, Evers came home late after a meeting with NAACP leaders; it was dark, he had a white shirt on, which was an easy target.

There was a shot.

Evers fell to the ground, shot in the back. He staggered 30 feet toward his home. The bullet went through him, through the house wall and was later found. He died in a local hospital 50 minutes later.

Police subsequently found the weapon, a Enfield 1917 rifle; *the shooter had left it in nearby bushes.* The Enfield was too common to trace, but a telescopic scope on the rifle was relatively rare; it was soon traced to Byron De La Beckwith.

Beckwith was arrested for murder. He went to trial. Twice. The first trial had an *all white male jury*; It deadlocked on a verdict. He was again tried for murder. The second trial also had an *all white male jury*. It too deadlocked on a verdict.

Beckwith went free until 1977, when he was imprisoned until 1980, for conspiring to murder one A.I. Botnick.

In 1994, Beckwith was again tried for murdering Evers, based on new DNA evidence. This time he was found guilty. He appealed, unsuccessfully.

Medgar Evers had served honorably in the U.S. Army and was buried at Arlington National Cemetery with full military honors.

... and ...

In 1992, the city of Jackson, Mississippi erected a statue in his honor;

All of Delta Drive, part of U.S. Highway 49 in Jackson, was named for him;

In 2004, the Jackson airport was renamed the Jackson-Medgar Wiley Evers International Airport;

A statue of him was subsequently erected on the campus of his alma mater, Alcorn State University;

In October, 2009, Navy Secretary Ray Mabus, a former Governor of the state of Mississippi, announced that the USNS Medgar Evers, a Lewis and Clark-class dry cargo ship, would be named in his honor;

The 1967 film, *Ghosts of Mississippi*, directed by Rob Reiner tells the story of the 1994 retrial of Byron De La Beckwith, based on the book of the same name by Maryanne Vollers;

Medgar Evers College, a senior college of the City University of New York, was established in Brooklyn in 1969-1970. It thrives today;

On the 50th anniversary of his death, a tribute was held in Arlington National Cemetery. Former President Bill Clinton,

Attorney General Eric Holder, Navy Secretary
Ray Mabus, Senator Roger Wicker, NAACP
President Ben Jealous and Evers' widow, Myrlie
Evers-Williams all paid tribute to Evers;
And there have been other honors.

As he had done with the Emmett Till murder, Bob
Dylan wrote, and has performed, a song about the
Evers murder, "Only A Pawn in Their Game." The lyrics
include:

> *The deputy sheriffs, the soldiers*
> *the governors get paid*
> *And the marshall and cops get the same*
> *But the poor white man's used in the hands of them*
> *all like a tool*
> *He's taught in his school*
> *From the start by the rule*
> *That the laws are with him*
> *To protect his white skin*
> *To keep up his hate*
> *So he never thinks straight*
> *'Bout the shape that he's in*
> *But it ain't him to blame.*
> *He's only a pawn in their game.*

Byron De La Beckwith died in prison, at 80, in
January, 2001.

Eight

1963: Fannie Lou Hamer

... sick and tired of being sick and tired ...

FANNIE LOU HAMER IS one of the nation's civil rights activists who should be more widely known and remembered.

She was born Fannie Lou Townsend October 17, 1917 in Montgomery County, Mississippi, the youngest of 20 children.

Twenty children; 14 boys and 6 girls. In 1919, her family moved to Sunflower County, Mississippi, so they could work on the plantation of E.W. Brandon. She picked cotton as a child and by 13 could pick 200-300 pounds per day.

In This Little Light of Mine: The life of Fannie Lou Hamer, biographer Kay Mills writes:

> Fannie Lou Hamer was poor and unlet-
> tered. She walked with a limp. A short, stocky

black woman, for much of her life she worked weighting the cotton picked on a white man's plantation in the heart of the Mississippi Delta.

She lived in a small frame house that had no hot water and no working indoor toilet—while her boss's dog had its own bathroom inside the main house. She had an earthy sense of humor, an ability to quote vast passages from the Bible, and the respect of those who knew her. They counted on her to straighten out disputes and intercede in the white community when necessary and knew that she and her husband, Pap, would take in children other families could not raise. She knew there was much wrong with America, but until the civil rights movement came to her town, she could do little about those wrongs.

And, Mills writes, "By almost any measure, black Mississippians had little share in the American Dream of opportunity as they entered the 1960s." And ...

She would lose her job, be jailed and beaten, for her beliefs. She symbolized one aspect of what the (civil rights) movement hoped to accomplish: to embolden local people to resist a harsh and violent system.

From this humblest of beginnings, Mrs. Hamer would go on to challenge the president of the United States, the national Democratic Party, members of Congress and the American people about fulfilling the promises of democracy. She recognized the shortcomings in the nation's electoral and education systems. She opposed the war in Vietnam from the beginning, and she was thrilled by seeing Africans govern themselves. She organized programs to feed poor people, tend to their ills, house them, clothe them, train them for jobs. She ran for office. She recognized the need for women of all races to work together for political and social goals. She encouraged young people to set and achieve their own goals.

* * *

She was not perfect, but she was, to many who worked with her under the most life-threatening conditions, the most inspirational person they ever knew.

* * *

She died poor because she gave away much of what she earned or raised.

School, such as it was for black children in Mississippi, stared in December, when the cotton was in, and ran through March. Fannie Lou excelled; she won spelling bees and recited poetry and sang. She left school after the sixth grade to help support her family. But she read and read, whatever and whenever she could.

She married in 1944; her husband Perry Hamer was 32; she was 27. They lived in a small home on a Ruleville plantation, with a toilet that was broken. The plantation owner refused to fix it. She worked cleaning the planation main house one day; after cleaning one bathroom she began cleaning another. The daughter of the planation owner told her, "You don't have to clean this one too good, Fannie Lou. It's just Old Honey's." Ole Honey was the family dog. "I just couldn't get over that dog having a bathroom when (the owner) wouldn't even have the toilet fixed for us. But then, Negroes in Mississippi are treated *worse* than dogs," she later said.

Like Rosa Parks, Fannie Lou Hamer was deeply religious. She joined the Strangers Home Baptist Church when she was 12 and was baptized in the Quiver River.

And she could sing. *She could sing.* Harry Belafonte sometimes sang with her, later, as did Pete Seeger. One of her favorites was "This Little Light of Mine."

Singing, she once said,

> is one of the main things that can keep us going. When you're in a brick cell, locked up, and haven't done anything to anybody but still you're locked up there are sometimes words just begin to come to you and you begin to sing. Like one of my favorite songs, "This Little Light of Mine, I'm Going to Let it Shine." This same song goes back to the fifth chapter of Matthew, which is the Beatitudes of the Bible, when he says a city that sets on a hill cannot be hid. Let your light so shine that men would see your good works and glorify the father which is in heaven. I think singing is very important. It brings out the soul.

In 1961, she went to a local hospital to have a small uterine tumor removed. Without her permission or knowledge, *she was sterilized*. It meant nothing to complain to the white doctor; and she would have risked her life trying to sue a white doctor in Mississippi.

It was the final indignity; she soon became an activist.

A year later, in August, 1962, Rev. James Bevel, an organizer for the Student Nonviolent Coordinating Committee (SNCC) and an associate of the Rev. Martin Luther King, Jr. gave a sermon in Ruleville and followed it an appeal for volunteers to register to vote. Everyone listening knew the consequences; you could lose your job, you could be beaten, you could be killed. Lynched. Fannie Lou Hamer volunteered.

"I guess if I'd had any sense, I'd have been a little scared—but what was the point of being scared? The only thing they could do was kill me, and it kinda seemed like they'd been trying to do that a little bit at a time to me since I could remember."

She was ideal for the emerging civil rights movement. As Kay Mills writes:

> Fannie Lou Hamer had a presence. She was smart. And as a poor black southern sharecropper, she represented the soul of the people whom the movement wanted to represent. As disenfranchised people were starting to assert themselves, she stepped forward, voicing her concerns and those of her neighbors. She had a personal story, which would only grow more

compelling the more she endured. And she had
a voice with which to tell it. Virtually everyone
whose path crossed hers remembered first and
foremost her singing and her speaking.

On a bus trip to Indianola, Mississippi, she bolstered
the spirits of other organizers by signing. "Go Tell It on
the Mountain," "We Shall Overcome," "This Little Light
of Mine," and other spirituals and hymns. SNCC leaders
told local organizers: "find the lady that sings."

Although she worked for the SNCC throughout the
south, she continued to live in Mississippi. And she lost
her job because of her organizing.

On June 3, 1963, she and others were returning
from a trip to Charleston, South Carolina, and stopped
in Winona, Mississippi, for a restroom break and perhaps coffee. Waitresses at the local cafe were outraged
that they wanted service. Police were quickly called. All
were taken to the local jail. The only male in the group,
James West was jailed with other male inmates.

June Johnson, then 15, was hit by a policeman.
Annell Ponder, also arrested, saw Johnson bleeding.
West was beaten by other inmates.

Hamer was ordered to lie face down on a cell bed.
Another inmate was ordered to beat her with a black-
jack—if he didn't he would be beaten. The inmate beat
her until he was exhausted. And then she was beaten
by another.

Her screams could be heard throughout the building. No one else was beaten as she was. June Johnson
later testified that neither she nor anyone else were

allowed medical treatment or telephone calls. Johnson said:

> The food was terrible, so we all ended up going on a strike. We would sing a lot of the songs, and (Mrs. Hamer's) particular song she would sing while in jail was "When Paul and Silas Were Bound in Jail." She still had a good spirit in spite of her (ordeal) but she really suffered in that jail from that beating. I mean, her body was black and her skin felt like—I don't know if you ever felt a snake skin but it would be rough, like it was raw cowhide.

Although friends and colleagues knew they were missing, no one could find them. They were finally taken to court Monday June 11. There were no charges against June Johnson as she was only 15, but the others were fined $65 each for disorderly conduct and $35 each for resisting arrest. They were released June 12 after Andrew Young posted their bail.

Hoover wired the FBI Memphis office to enter the case. Records extant now do not indicate how efficient or enthusiastic the FBI might have been in the case, but archived records do show Attorney General Robert Kennedy knew of the case.

The Justice Department eventually filed both civil and criminal charges. The jury in the case against the policemen was an all-white jury. Sol Poe, then an inmate at the Parchman Penitentiary, testified he was forced to beat her.

In jury deliberations that lasted scarcely over an hour, the policemen in the case were all found not guilty.

It took Fannie Lou Hamer a full month to recover in a hospital from her injuries. It may well be said she never really recovered.

She then continued her struggle for basic human rights in Mississippi and in the south.

She was interviewed by Jamie DeMuth for an article in *The Nation* magazine. "All of my life I've been sick and tired. Now I'm sick and tired of being sick and tired."

The slogan caught on. Later, when she attended conventions or meetings, others would see her and chant the lines, "I'm sick and tired of being sick and tired."

In 1964, Hamer and others challenged the all-white Mississippi state delegation to the National Democratic convention, set to nominate Lyndon Johnson for re-election as President. The state delegation was not representative of all Mississippi Democrats, she and others rightly charged. Johnson, speaking privately to his inner circle, called her "that illiterate woman."

He wanted no side issue to interrupt the nomination process. She and other protestors were offered a compromise in seating Mississippi delegates. They thought it unfair.

Johnson called a press conference the next day on another topic to change national attention from the convention seating problem. Eventually a second compromise was accepted without her participation or input.

In 1968, the National Democratic party adopted a convention rule guaranteeing fair seating for all state delegates.

Fannie Lou Hamer continued her civil rights activities.

She died March 14, 1977, in Mount Bayou, Mississippi, at 59, of heart failure, brought on by hypertension. U.N. Ambassador Andrew Young spoke the eulogy at her services.

There is now a Memorial Garden in Ruleville, Mississipi, named for her; it also includes a statue of her. Her gravestone, in Ruleville, carries the following inscription:

FANNIE LOU HAMER

OCTOBER 6, 1917

MARCH 14, 1977

I AM SICK AND TIRED

OF BEING

SICK AND TIRED

Nine

1965: Malcolm X

Murdered in New York City, February 21, 1965

Age: 39

IN HIS TIME, HE was the most polarizing and controversial figure in American Civil Rights. Some saw him as a positive influence on civil rights; others saw a *hate whitey* attitude, black supremacy and a continuing incitement to violence.

In the Introduction to *The Autobiography of Malcolm X*, journalist M. S. Handler wrote:

> His public performances on television and in meeting halls produced an almost terrifying effect. His implacable marshaling of facts and his logic had something of a new dialectic, diabolic in its force. He frightened white television audiences, demolished his Negro opponents, but elicited a remarkable response from Negro audiences. Many Negro opponents in the end

refused to make any public appearances on the same platform with him. The troubled white audiences were confused, disturbed, felt themselves threatened. Some began to consider Malcolm evil incarnate.

Malcolm appealed to the two most disparate elements in the Negro community—the depressed mass, and the galaxy of Negro writers and artists who have burst on the American scene in the past decade. The Negro middle class—the Negro "establishment"—abhorred and feared Malcolm as much as he despised it.

The impoverished Negroes respected Malcolm in the way that wayward children respect the grandfather image. It was always a strange and moving experience to walk with Malcolm in Harlem. He was known to all. People glanced shyly. Sometimes Negro children would ask for his autograph.

He was born Malcolm Little, in Omaha, Nebraska, May 19, 1925. His father Earl Little was a Baptist lay speaker and local leader of the Universal Negro Improvement Association, which encouraged self-reliance and black pride. The family moved to Milwaukee in 1926 and then to Lansing, Michigan. When he was six, his father died when he fell or was pushed in front of a streetcar. Some believed it was a suicide; Malcolm later believed he was pushed by a member or members of the Black Legion, a white supremacy group.

In 1938, his mother had a nervous breakdown and was set to the Kalamazoo State Hospital. Malcolm and his siblings got her out—24 years later.

He wanted to become a lawyer, but a white teacher told him that was "no realistic goal for a nigger." Although he had otherwise done well, he then dropped out of junior high school, after the eighth grade.

At 15, he moved to Boston where he had a half-sister.

In 1943, he moved to Harlem, where he was involved in gambling, racketeering, robbery and pimping.

He was a street hustler, pure and simple. Anything for money, for sex, for entertainment. His nickname was "Detroit Red," because of the red hair he had inherited from a Scottish grandmother. And he was declared "mentally unqualified for military service," after he told a psychiatrist, "I want to get sent down South. Organize them black soldiers, you dig? Steal us some guns, and kill up crackers."

He returned to Boston in late 1945 and began a string of burglaries. In 1946, he was arrested and in February, began a ten year sentence at Charlestown State Prison, a horror that had been built in 1805, and, he wrote, was even patterned after the Bastille.

Prison changed his life.

He was transfered to Concord Prison and while there got a letter from his brother Philbert, who told him about "the Nation of Islam." In 1948, through the efforts of his sister Ella, he was then transfered to the Norfolk, Massachusetts, Prison Colony, virtually a university with walls. Its library, Malcolm stated, had thousands of books.

The Nation of Islam and the prison books ... those were his two obsessions. Detroit Red, the street hustler disappeared.

He finally had an education. He read Will Durant's *Story of Civilization*; H. G. Wells' *Outline of History*; *Souls of Black Folk*; Carter G. Woodson's *Negro History*; J.A. Rogers' three-volume set *Sex and Race*; Herodotus; Gandhi ..., race relations, ancient history, black culture, philosophy ... "Ten guards and the warden couldn't have torn me out of those books," he later said. He read so much in the dark he sustained permanent eye damage.

(Much later, during an interview, he was asked, "What's your alma mater?"

"Books," he said.)

He learned more and more about the Nation of Islam and its leader Elijah Muhammad. He finally wrote a one-page letter to Muhammad; Muhammad urged him to pray, but it took one week for Malcolm to will himself to bend his knees and pray. He became a member of the Nation of Islam in prison.

After beginning his correspondence with Muhammad, he became content in prison. "Between Mr. Muhammad's teachings, my correspondence, my visitors ... and my reading of books, months passed without my even thinking about being imprisoned. In fact, up to then, I had never been so truly free in my life."

In 1950 he changed his name to Malcolm X; the X signifying an African family name he never could know and that his former name Little, a slave name imposed on him. (The X also signified what he had become, he later said: Ex-smoker. Ex-drinker. Ex-christian. Ex-slave.) He also used the name El-Hajj Malik El-Shabazz

When he was released on parole in 1952, he visited Elijah Muhammad in Chicago and joined the Nation of

Islam. He was named assistant minister of the Nation's Temple Number One in Detroit; later that same year he established Boston's Temple Number 11, later expanded Temple Number 12 in Philadelphia and was then selected to lead Temple Number Seven in Harlem.

He practiced the Nation of Islam's spartan beliefs: no drinking; no smoking; no drugs; no sexual license or even dating; no dances or ballgames or movies; no sleeping late; no more than one meal a day. He wouldn't even go to his friend Ossie Davis's Broadway play *Purlie Victorious* without a special dispensation from Elijah Muhammad.

He had written to President Harry Truman in 1950, protesting the Korean War and declaring himself a communist. By 1953, J. Edgar Hoover's FBI was conducting surveillance on him, as they also would on Martin Luther King, Jr., when he became nationally prominent.

Seeking souls for The Nation of Islam in Harlem was no small task. But, as Peter Goldman writes, *he never lived there*—Malcolm X always *commuted* to work there:

> Malcolm listened and learned, and with his fishers- for-souls worked the edges of other people's crowds for converts to his struggling temple. They worked the church doors as well, and the carryout shops and poolrooms and backstreets—anywhere black people were—and gradually, inchmeal, built the communion of the Original People in Harlem from a few dozen to a few hundred regular followers.

Malcolm worked Harlem but he never came back there to live—not even during those first uncertain days when he was single and scuffing by on whatever came back into the collection buckets. As a hustler years before, he had lived downtown when he could, bunking for a time with "a friend" on Park Avenue. ("I had to go through the service entrance," he remembered wryly, "and make believe I was a delivery boy") and for another period of time in his own pad in Greenwich Village. When he returned as a Muslim, something held him back from that last symbolic commitment of the pastor to his parish. Perhaps it was he sensibility of the Nation, perhaps Malcolm's own upwardly mobile reach for respect; in any case, he took a furnished room in the black inner suburbs, in a brother Muslim's house in East Elmhurst, Long Island. Increasing prosperity regularized his income; the temple put him on a base allowance of $125 (and later $150) a week plus anything more he needed for traveling and propagating the faith. Prosperity upgraded his housing, too; he moved out of his single room to three rooms in a two-family flat—and later, after he married and began having children to a seven-room home of his own. But Malcolm never left East Elmhurst; he was a commuter to Harlem until the day he died.

Journalist Mike Wallace did a week-long television special about the Nation of Islam, but it was a double-edged sword. It gave the Nation of Islam visibility, but many viewers believed it was simply a *hate whitey* movement. Newspaper and magazine articles soon followed, but Malcolm X eclipsed Elijah Muhammad. Malcolm X was the face and the spokesman for the Nation of Islam. He was invited to speak at Harvard (four times, he proudly said), at Wellesley, Simmons, Boston University, Wesleyan, Rutgers ... a supreme achievement for a street hustler with a prison education.

Malcolm X claimed there were 40,000 Nation of Islam members in Harlem; critics said maybe 10,000 at the peak of the movement. Maybe 10,000. A key problem was that he was a firebrand, for good or otherwise; but he never got anyone a job or found anyone an apartment.

Whites could see that the old-time segregation was eroding in the south, perhaps more slowly than anyone wanted, but progress was being made. Malcolm X's rhetoric was something many simply could not conceive:

> These aren't white people. You're not using the right language when you say the white man. You call it the devil. When you call him the devil, you're calling him by his name, and he's got another name—Satan; another name—serpent; another name—snake; another name—beast. All those names are in the Bible for the white man. Another name—Pharaoh; another name—Caesar; another name—France; another name—French; Frenchmen; Englishmen; American; all these are just names for the devil.

And, he said,

> Historically, I think, the weight of the evidence is against them if you're looking for angelic deeds.

And ...

> If you'll notice, whenever I refer to America, I don't say *we*. I don't say *I* or *our*. I say *you*. This is *yours*, it's not *me* or *mine*. And you'll find that this thinking is increasing among black people today. They don't say *our* government, *our* President, *our* Senate, *our* Congress, nor do they say *our* troubles. They say *your* President, *your* Congress, *your* Senate—and *your* troubles.

His rhetoric was absolute. Once, at Adam Clayton Powell's Baptist Church in Harlem, he was asked about the hate issue.

> How can anybody ask us do we hate the white man who kidnapped us four hundred years ago, brought us here and stripped us of our history, stripped us of our culture, stripped us of our language, striped us of everything you could have used today to prove you're part of the human family, bring you down to the level of an animal, sell you from plantation to plantation like a sack of wheat, sell you like a sack of potatoes, sell you like a horse and a plow, and

then hung you up from one end of the country
to the other, and then you ask me do I hate him?
Why, your question is worthless.

Martin Luther King, Jr. had conflicting views about
him. King told *Playboy* magazine interviewer Alex
Haley:

He is very articulate ... but I totally disagree
with many of his political and philosophical
views ... I don't want to seem to sound self-
righteous, ... or that I think I have the only
truth, the only way. Maybe he does have some
of the answer .... I have often wished that he
would talk less of violence, because violence is
not going to solve our problem. And in his litany
of articulating the despair of the Negro without
offering any positive, creative alternative, I feel
that Malcolm has done himself a disservice ....
Urging Negroes to arm themselves and prepare
to engage in violence, as he has done, can reap
nothing but grief.

Malcolm X was a member of the Nation of Islam for
a decade, but the civil rights struggle increasingly be-
longed to Martin Luther King, Jr. and his philosophy
of non-violence. It did not help his cause when he de-
nounced the March on Washington, which included
Martin Luther King, Jr.'s "I Have a Dream" speech,
now widely considered one of the greatest American
speeches of all time.

"This is nothing but a circus, nothing but a picnic," he said.

He was offered a book contract by Doubleday with a author royalty advance of $20,000. Doubleday later dropped the book project and Grove Press, the most avant-garde (and left-leaning) publisher of the time, took it. *The Autobiography of Malcolm X* sold 25,000 copies in hardcover and over million copies in paperback within five years.

Malcolm X left the Nation of Islam in March 1964; he eventually became a Sunni Muslim. He traveled in Africa and the Middle East, then returned to form Muslim Mosque, Inc. and the Organization of Afro-American Unity, but then—nothing. He could not duplicate the recruiting successes he had achieved earlier and he knew that when he left the Nation of Islam, he had left behind sworn enemies.

He was scheduled to speak February 21, 1965 at the Audubon Ballroom, in New York.

Peter Goldman writes:

> At the end, death was closing in on him and everybody saw it. The police saw it: two weeks before the event, the top command received an intelligence estimate that he was in imminent danger and offered him round-the-clock protection, knowing he would never accept. His friends saw it: they begged him to get out of town for a while—to Africa, to Europe, to California, anywhere away from Harlem and the most visible of his enemies. And Malcolm X saw it. He told

people he didn't care really, not for himself, but he lived out his last weeks and months jumping at street sounds and flinching at shadows, and that the end some of the brothers worried that he might be cracking. "He really got strung out .... He wanted to die. Malcolm *wanted* to die." One cannot easily imagine a man so alive embracing death. Yet the desperation of those days finally did seem to push him past caring, and if he did not want to die, he was too spent to run from death any longer.

As he began to speak in the Audubon Ballroom, a blast from a double-barreled sawed-off shotgun hit him in the chest; two other gunmen using semi-automatic handguns also hit him several times. An autopsy found 21 gunshot wounds; 10 of the wounds were from buckshot to his left chest and shoulder from the shotgun. The assailants were later identified as Talmadge Heyer, Norman 3X Butler and Thomas 15X Johnson, all members of the Nation of Islam.

Actor and activist Ossie Davis gave the eulogy at his funeral.

Since his death, there have been streets named after him: in Harlem; Brooklyn; Dallas; Lansing, Michigan; schools have been named after him in Newark, New Jersey; Madison, Wisconsin; Chicago, and elsewhere. The Malcolm X Library and Performing Arts Center, a part of the San Diego Public Library system, was opened in 1996. Columbia University opened the Malcolm X and Dr. Betty Shabazz Memorial and Educational Center, in 2005.

Denzel Washington played the title role in the film *Malcolm X*, released in 1992, an adoption of his book, *The Autobiography of Malcolm X*. And there have been seven other theater films or made-for-television films about Malcolm X.

The United States Postal Service issued a Malcolm X postage stamp in 1999.

One of the assailants, Norman 3X Butler, now known as Muhammad Abdul Aziz, was paroled in 1985; Thomas 15X Johnson, converted to Sunni Islam while in prison. He maintained his innocence until his death in 2009; Talmadge Hayer, one of the assailants, now known as Mujahid Halim, was paroled in 2010.

Ten |

1968: Martin Luther King, Jr.

Murdered in Memphis, Tennessee, April 4, 1968
Age: 39

HE WAS 25 WHEN he entered a meeting—late—of Montgomery, Alabama, black church leaders who were searching for methods, and a civic leader, to aid Rosa Parks, arrested for refusing to give up her seat on the Montgomery bus.

"I'm not a coward," he said, "I don't want anyone to call me a coward." He was chosen, that night, to become the leader; much later, in *Stride Toward Freedom: The Montgomery Story*, he wrote:

> As I thought further I came to see that what
> we were really doing was withdrawing our coop-
> eration from an evil system, rather than merely
> withdrawing our economic support from the

bus company. The bus company, being an external expression of the system, would naturally suffer, but the basic aim was to refuse to cooperate with evil. At this point I began to think about Thoreau's *Essay on Civil Disobedience*. I remember how, as a college student, I had been moved when I first read this work. I became convinced that what we were preparing to do in Montgomery was related to what Thoreau had expressed. We were simply saying to the white community. "We can no longer lend our cooperation to an evil system."

Something began to say to me, "He who passively accepts evil is as much involved in it as he who helps perpetrate it. He who accepts evil without protesting against it is really accepting cooperation with it." When oppressed people willingly accept their oppression they only serve to give the oppressor a convenient justification for his acts. Often the oppressor goes along unaware of the evil involved in his oppression so long as the oppressed accept it. So in order to be true to one's conscience and true to God, a righteous man has no alternative but to refuse to cooperate with an evil system. This I felt was the nature of our action. From this moment on I conceived of our movement as an act of massive noncooperation, From then on I rarely used the word "boycott."

In August, 1953, before the Montgomery bus boycott, Martin Luther King, Jr. had been in school, by his own count, twenty-two years without a break. He attended Booker T. Washington High school in Atlanta and entered Morehouse College, in Atlanta, at 15 without formally graduating from high school. He obtained a B.A. degree from Morehouse College; a Bachelor's of Divinity degree from Crozer Theological Seminary, in Chester, Pennsylvania, and had completed all the coursework and the residency requirements for a doctorate at Boston University.

Two major influences during his academic career were Gandhi and Thoreau.

He married Coretta Scott on June 18, 1953 in her hometown of Heiberger, Alabama. They eventually had four children: Yolanda; Martin Luther King III; Dexter and Bernice.

While completing his work at Boston University, King had several offers; pastorates in the north and the south, teaching or administrative positions at three universities.

He was offered an opportunity to preach a sermon at the Dexter Avenue Baptist Church in Montgomery. He did so and was subsequently offered the pastorate there in 1954, which he accepted. He completed his doctorate at Boston University in June, 1955.

Thus the boycott began, although they all knew a boycott was illegal in Alabama, by state law. King also said:

> But there comes a time when people get tired of being trampled by oppression. There come a time when people get tired of being

plunged into the abyss of exploitation and nagging injustice. The story of Montgomery is the story of 50,000 such Negroes who were willing to substitute tired feet for tired souls, and walk the streets of Montgomery until the walls of segregation were finally battered by the forces of justice.

Martin Luther King, Jr. fervently believed in nonviolence. As he wrote in *Stride Toward Freedom*:

> ... Montgomery's Negroes showed themselves willing to grapple with a new approach to the crisis in race relations. It is probably true that most of them did not believe in nonviolence as a philosophy of life, but because of their confidence in their leaders and because nonviolence was presented to them as a simple expression of Christianity in action, they were willing to use it as a technique.

He had to hold press conferences as often as three times a week during the bus boycott. It finally ended in victory 381 days after it began and, by the end, two names were nationally known: Rosa Parks and Martin Luther King, Jr.

But, as a foreshadowing of violence to come, during the boycott his house was bombed. Both he and Parks—and others—received death threats.

In 1957, King, along with Ralph Abernathy, Fred Shuttlesworth and other clergy formed the Southern

Christian Leadership Conference (SCLC), to energize and involve black clergy and black churches, to conduct non-violent demonstrations and to provide a vehicle for civil rights. Martin Luther King, Jr. led the SCLC until his death. Abernathy and many others became nearly as famous as King, and suffered the same for their beliefs; *they* were arrested, *they* received hate mail and death threats, *their* homes were bombed, *their* churches were bombs. None were dissuaded.

In 1963, Attorney General Robert Kennedy, doubtlessly at the urging of J. Edgar Hoover began an FBI investigation of King. Hoover—and perhaps Kennedy—believed the SCLC was infiltrated by communists. Kennedy authorized Hoover to wire-tap King and other SCLC leaders. The hunt for communists in the SCLC came to nothing but the surveillance continued. The FBI even sent anonymous letters to King, urging him to commit suicide. One read, in part:

> The American public, the church organizations that have been helping—Protestants, Catholics and Jews will know you for what you are—an evil beast. So will others who have backed you. You are done. King, there is only one thing left for you to do. You know what it is. You have just 34 days in which to do (this exact number has been selected for a specific reason, it has definite practical significant [sic]}. You are done. There is but one way out for you. You better take it before your filthy fraudulent self is bared to the nation.

Hoover also once called King "the most notorious liar in the country."

Hoover, FBI director-for-life, had a scandalously long and sordid record of improper FBI investigations. Among those the FBI followed, and had files on, were: novelists Ernest Hemingway and John Steinbeck (the files on Steinbeck continued even after his death in December, 1968); Charlie Chapin (the FBI believed he was a communist); Eleanor Roosevelt; Jackie Robinson (he too, was suspected of being a communist); Paul Robeson; Thurgood Marshall and W.E.B. DuBois, of the NAACP. More recently, the FBI also maintained files on Cesar Chavez and the United Farm Workers (over 2,000 pages of files); the Black Panther Party; the Beatles; John Lennon (a separate file); Hugh Hefner, publisher of *Playboy* magazine (he had been critical of the FBI); and activist Abbie Hoffman, among others. Since the death of Hoover, no one is allowed to stay in office as FBI Director for more than ten years.

In spring, 1963, the SCLC began a campaign against segregation and injustice in Birmingham, Alabama. At first the protests did not succeed. During the protests, Birmingham Police, under the direction of Chief Eugene "Bull" Connor, knocked demonstrators to the streets with high-pressure water cannons and set attack dogs on them. Shown nationally on the evening news, viewers throughout the country were horrified. *Bull Connor* became synonymous with *police brutality*. President John Kennedy saw a picture of a police dog lunging at a black woman and said it made him "sick." Martin Luther King, Jr. was arrested—for the 13th time. (He was eventually arrested *29 times*.) Taken to the Birmingham jail, he wrote a "Letter from the Birmingham Jail" on scraps of paper, smuggled out of the jail and retyped.

Eight white Alabama ministers had previously urged King to continue the civil rights struggles in the courts, but not in the streets.

In the Birmingham Jail letter, he wrote:

> I had hoped that the white moderate would understand that law and order exist for the purpose of establishing justice, and that when they fail to do this they become dangerously structured dams that block the flow of social progress. I had hoped that the white moderate would understand that the present tension of the South is merely a necessary phase of the transition from an obnoxious negative peace, where the Negro passively accepted his unjust plight, to a substance-filled positive peace, where all men will respect the dignity and worth of human personality. Actually, we who engage in nonviolent direct action are not the creators of tension. We merely bring to the surface the hidden tension that is already alive. We bring it out into the open where it can be seen and dealt with. Like a boil that can never be cured as long as it is covered up but must be opened with all its pus-flowing ugliness to the natural medicines of air and light, injustice must likewise be exposed, with all of the tension its exposing creates, to the light of human conscience and the air of national opinion before it can be cured.

And, he wrote ...

> I just close now. But before closing I am impelled to mention one other point in your statement that troubled me profoundly. You warmly commended the Birmingham police for keeping "order" and "preventing violence." I don't believe you would have been so warmly commended the police force if you had seen its angry violent dogs literally biting six unarmed, nonviolent Negroes. I don't believe you would so quickly commend the policemen if you would observe their ugly and inhuman treatment of Negroes here in the city jail; if you would watch them push and curse old Negro women and young Negro girls; if you would see them slap and kick old Negro men and young boys; if you would observe them, as they did on two occasions refuse to give us food because we wanted to say our grace together. I'm sorry that I can't join you in your praise for the police department.

By the early 1960s there were six organizations all fighting for racial justice. They, and their leaders were: the National Association for the Advancement of Colored People, Roy Wilkins; the National Urban League, Whitney Young; the Brotherhood of Sleeping Car Porters, A. Philip Randolph; SNCC, John Lewis; the Congress of Racial Equality, James Farmer, Jr. and the Southern Christian Leadership Conference, Martin Luther King, Jr.

They met and decided to set a March on Washington for August 28, 1963. They advised President John Kennedy of their intentions; he initially opposed the idea, but relented and helped support it. He also encouraged other churches and the United Auto Workers to support the march. The first estimates were that 100,000 might attend. Malcolm X issued an order forbidding Nation of Islam members from attending.

Little is remembered now of the issues involved. The rally demanded: an end to racial segregation in schools; meaningful civil rights legislation; a law banning racial discrimination in hiring; protection from police brutality; a $2 minimum wage (a $2 minimum wage—in 1963!); and self-government for Washington, D.C. (which to this day has not yet been achieved).

The 1963 March on Washington is now largely remembered only for Martin Luther King, Jr.'s speech, "I Have a Dream," and the size of the audience, a record then.

All exceptional writers "collect" words, phrases, incidents and anecdotes for their eventual use. (John Steinbeck, it is believed, wrote *Of Mice and Men*, 1937, based on a similar incident he heard about in California when he was living in the Salinas area. And his first wife gave him the title to his epic Depression-era novel, *The Grapes of Wrath*, 1939, which was a line in "The Battle Hymn of the Republic," by Julia Ward Howe.)

In fact, King's speech was not written solely for the March; he knew of the line "I Have a Dream" earlier and used basically the same speech in local situations, before that time.

In *The Dream: Martin Luther King, Jr., and The Speech That Inspired a Nation*, Drew Hansen writes ...

> One possibility is that King heard "I Have a Dream" from someone in Albany, Georgia in 1961-62. There are two stories that explain how this might have happened. King may have heard Prathia Hall, a young SNCC worker say "I have a dream" several times during a prayer service on September 14, 1962 at the remains of the Mount Olive Baptist Church in Sasser, Georgia, after it had been burned to the ground by segregationists.

Or, Hansen writes, other SNCC workers were also using it about that time and he may have picked it up from one of them ...

Or, another possibility is that he took it from The Bible. Hansen also writes:

> The Biblical resonances in King's "I Have a Dream" set pieces are so dense that the Bible must have influenced King's construction. The antecedents to "I Have a Dream" in King's own oratory are so clearly dependent on Biblical sources. It may never be possible to identify with certainty the sources of the "I Have a Dream" refrain, but given the theme's prominence in scripture and its precedents in King's own oratory, it is probable that King drew the phrase, as he had drawn so much of his language, from the King James translation of the Bible.

In short, Martin Luther King, Jr. had developed much of his "I Have a Dream" theme and his speech much earlier and had presented it, in various forms, at churches and meetings before that time.

To say the government was fearful of the March is a vast understatement. As Hansen writes:

> The police presence that day turned downtown Washington into one of the most heavily guarded places in America: at dawn police blockaded one hundred blocks in the center of the city. Thirteen cranes borrowed from the army, stood ready to tow broken-down buses at the mall. Police officers and members of the National Guard were posted on every corner. Additional squads of military and civil police provided protection for the congressional buildings. MPs in Jeeps and command cars patrolled downtown. There were so many soldiers on the streets one senator remarked that it looked as though a military coup had happened during the night. The army informed the FBI that it had seventeen thousand combat-ready troops stationed near Washington, and that forty-nine helicopters, some equipped with riot control munitions, had been put on standby at Fort Myer and Bolling Air Force Base, ready to descend on the nation's capital in the event of a riot.

Estimates of the crowd at the March on Washington were wildly wrong. Instead of 100,000, *more than*

250,000 people attended, from the steps of the Lincoln Memorial, onto the National Mall and around the Reflecting Pool. The folk group Peter, Paul and Mary sang to the crowd, as did Joan Baez, and there were other speakers, including John Lewis. Mahalia Jackson also sang to the crowd. Then Martin Luther King, Jr. was introduced. His speech was 17 minutes long. The "I Have a Dream" theme occurred about two-thirds toward the end:

> *I say to you today, my friends, so even though we face the difficult times of today and tomorrow, I still have a dream. It is deeply rooted in the American dream.*
>
> *I have a dream that one day this nation will rise up and live out the true meaning of its creed: "We hold these truths to be self-evident: that all men are created equal."*
>
> *I have a dream that one day on the red hills of Georgia the sons of former slaves and the sons of former slave owners will be able to sit down together at the table of brotherhood.*
>
> *I have a dream that one day even the state of Mississippi, a state sweltering with the heat of oppression, will be transformed into an oasis of freedom and justice.*
>
> *I have a dream today that my four little children will one day live in a nation where they will not be judged by the color of their skin, but by the content of their character.*
>
> *I have a dream today ....*

It was not so much a speech as a sermon; a sermon that he could have given at his own Dexter Avenue Baptist Church, and did give, with some variations, at other churches before the Washington march. It was a sermon given in the style and delivery of southern black ministers and for those not from the south, who had never heard King, it was electric. It was rich with the tones and cadences of the King James Bible and the belief that their cause was right.

Weldon Johnson published an Introduction to the 1927 book, *God's Trombones*. He could have been speaking about Martin Luther King, Jr.:

> The old-time Negro preacher ... was above all an orator, and in good measure an actor. He knew the secret of oratory, and that at bottom it is a progression of rhythmic words more than it is anything else .... He was a master of all the modes of eloquence. He often possessed a voice that was a marvelous instrument, a voice he could modulate from a sepulchral whisper to a crashing thunder clap. His discourse was generally kept at a high pitch of fervency, but occasionally he dropped into colloquialisms and less often, into humor .... His imagination was bold and unfettered. He had the power to sweep his hearers before him; and so himself was often swept away. At such times his language was not prose but poetry.

His "I Have a Dream" speech is now considered the best speech by an American in the twentieth century; many believe it rivals, and has the impact of, Lincoln's "Gettysburg Address."

It surely helped facilitate the passing of the Civil Rights Act of 1964 and the 1965 Voting Rights Act.

After the March, the struggle for equality continued.

In March, 1965, plans were made for a Selma, Alabama, to Montgomery protest march. It began March 7, ended in bloody violence as civil rights marchers were savagely beaten by Alabama police. Television shots of the beatings shocked—and enraged—viewers across the country and the march became known as "Bloody Sunday." A second march, scheduled for March 9 was aborted at King's request, but a third attempt, March 25, ended at the state capital in Montgomery. During a subsequent speech titled "How Long, Not Long," King used a phrase now one of the most frequently quoted about the civil rights era: "the arc of the moral universe is long, but it bends toward freedom."

In 1965, King also began to doubt the war in Vietnam. He spoke about the injustice of that war in New York City and elsewhere. He not only thought the war morally wrong, but that it also took funds and supplies away from the needy in the United States. "A nation that continues year after year to spend more money on military defense than on programs of social uplift is approaching spiritual death," he said. He continued to broaden his concerns—to include all social welfare concerns and injustices throughout the United States.

Chronicle of a Death Foretold
—1983 novel by Gabriel Garcia Márquez

On March 29, 1968 King traveled to Memphis to support black sanitation workers, represented by AFSCME Local 1733, which had been on strike for 17 days for better working conditions.

His plane had been delayed by a bomb threat, King said, in an April 3, address in Memphis. Referring to the bomb threat, he said:

> And then I got to Memphis. And some began to say the threats, or talk about the threats that were out. What would hFappen to me from some of our sick white brothers? Well, I don't know what will happen now. We've got some difficult days ahead. But it doesn't matter to me now. Because I've been to the mountaintop. And I don't mind. Like anybody, I would like to live a long life. Longevity has its place. But I'm not concerned about that now. I just want to do God's will. And He's allowed me to go up to the mountain. And I've looked over. And I've seen the promised land. I may not get there with you. But I want you to know tonight, that we, as a people, will get to the promised land. So I'm happy, tonight. I'm not worried about anything. I'm not fearing any man. Mine eyes have seen the glory of the coming of the Lord.

I may not get there with you .... shocked and stunned his audience. Was it his own *chronicle of a death foretold?*

In the book *April 4, 1968: Martin Luther King, Jr's Death and How It Changed America*, Michael Eric Dyson writes:

> You cannot hear the name Martin Luther King, Jr. and not think of death. You might hear the words "I Have a Dream," but they will doubtlessly only serve to underscore an image of a simple motel balcony, a large man made small, a pool of blood. For as famous as he may have been in life it is, and was, death that ultimately defined him. Born into a people whose main solace was Christianity's Promised Land awaiting them after the suffering of this world, King took on the power of his race's presumed destiny and found in himself the defiance necessary to spark change. He ate, drank, and slept death. He danced with it, he preached it, he feared it, and he stared it down. He looked for ways to lay it aside, this burden of his own mortality, but ultimately knew that his unwavering insistence on a nonviolent end to the mistreatment of his people would end violently.

He was standing on the second floor balcony of Memphis's Lorraine Motel, at 6:01 p.m. April 4, 1968, when one shot was fired. He slumped to the floor. The first on the scene were police. How did they arrive so quickly? They had King under surveillance—eye-sight distance surveillance from nearby.

He was rushed to Memphis's St. Joseph Hospital. A bullet had hit his right jaw, and traveled down his spinal cord and lodged in his shoulder. He was pronounced dead at 7:05 p.m. An autopsy later revealed that although he died at 39, he had the heart of a 60-year-old, prematurely aged by the stress of his civil rights work, biographer Taylor Branch has said.

President Lyndon Johnson declared April 7, a day of national mourning. But, following King's assassination, there were race riots throughout the country: in Washington, D.C.; Chicago; Baltimore; Louisville; Kansas City and many other cities.

Memphis soon settled the sanitation workers' strike in terms favorable to them.

Two months later, James Earl Ray was apprehended at the London, England, airport, where he was allegedly trying to reach white-ruled South Africa, by using a false Canadian passport. Ray had previous criminal convictions: for a burglary in California in 1949; armed robbery in Illinois in 1952; mail fraud in Missouri and armed robbery in St. Louis. He also used the alias Eric Starvo Galt.

Returned to Tennessee, he entered a guilty plea to the King killing, to avoid a death sentence. His sentence was 99 years in prison. He later attempted to recant the confession, ultimately unsuccessfully. William Bradford Huie, of the Emmett Till case, paid him to tell his story; Ray said that he wanted to kill King to be known as a "famous criminal."

Martin Luther King, Jr. was awarded at least 50 honorary university degrees and the Nobel Peace Prize in 1964, when he was 35.

After his death, President Jimmy Carter awarded him the President Medal of Freedom, in 1977; and he also received, posthumously, the Congressional Gold Medal in 2004. More than 730 cities throughout the country have named streets after him; in 1980 the U.S. Department of the Interior designed King's boyhood home and nearby areas a National Historic Site; King County, Washington rededicated its name in his honor and its logo now has his image on it; there is now a King Memorial on the National Mall in Washington, D.C. He is remembered as a martyr by the Episcopal Church in the United States and the Evangelical Lutheran Church.

The King Center, in Atlanta, established in 1968, is a 23-acre National Historic Site, which includes Dr. King's papers and archives and the tomb of Dr. King and his wife, Coretta Scott King, who died in 2006. At least one million people a year visit the Center.

His birthday is now a National Holiday.

James Earl Ray once escaped from the Tennessee State Prison and was recaptured three days later. One year was added to his sentence for a total of 100 years. He died in prison in April 1998, at 70. He was cremated. His ashes are nowhere to be found in the United States; they were sent to Ireland, his family's ancestral home.

Eleven |

1969: Grace Halsell

Soul Sister ...

THE THIRD BOOK IN the unofficial trilogy that began with *In The Land of Jim Crow* and continued with
Black Like Me, is Grace Halsell's *Soul Sister*, published
in 1969, eight years after *Black Like Me*. John Howard
Griffin never read *In the Land of Jim Crow*; it was published during his decade of blindness. He had books
read to him during that period, but they were largely
books picked for him by philosopher Jacques Maritain
and Father Stanley Murphy of Canada, founder of The
Christian Culture series.

And for a time, Grace Halsell missed reading *Black
Like Me*.

Like Griffin, Halsell was a native Texan. She stud-
ied at Texas Tech University from 1939 to 1942, at
Columbia University from 1943 into 1944, at Texas
Christian University from 1945 to 1951, and at the
Sorbonne from 1957-1958.

During those years she also worked for newspapers including the *Lubbock Avalanche-Journal*, the *Fort Worth Star-Telegram* and the Washington bureau of the *Houston Post*.

She covered the Korean War and later, the Vietnam War as a reporter. From 1965 to 1968 she worked as a White House speech writer for Lyndon Johnson.

She first heard of *Black Like Me* when she was working for Johnson.

> The title meant nothing to me. Perhaps I was in Turkey, Korea or Arabia when the book came out. And I hadn't heard of the author John Howard Griffin although we came from the same town, Fort Worth, Texas. The next day I bought *Black Like Me* and plunged into it, discovering Griffin talked to me like an inner voice, calm, suggestive. "I could do that ... I could be black."

She became fascinated, even obsessed with the idea. *She could be black too*, like Griffin. She experienced, even before becoming black, the same doppelgänger effect Griffin experienced.

> The seed is planted, it grows. I have not reasoned it there nor nourished it logically. Imagination, feeling, cause it to grow. (And what makes men different could be feeling rather than reason.) I had only to imagine myself black and then, for the first time, I saw myself white! This puzzled me, unsettled me.

* * *

Most white people still think of Negroes as somehow different and apart. They see their skin and nothing else. The depths of sensitivity, attitudes, abilities, emotions escape this superficial, subliminal view. I wanted to write a story revealing how much alike we all are. And I wanted to do it directly, from the most personal experience, so that I could actually feel the commonality and communicate it to others.

Halsell arranged to meet John Howard Griffin in Baltimore, where he was giving a speech, then they could drive to Washington, D.C., getting acquainted and he could take a plane out of Washington. They ate dinner in her apartment and she gave him a memo of what she planned to do.

He read it quietly, and with great feeling responded immediately: "Oh yes, you have to do it."

Griffin said he had always wished a woman could do what he had done, because there were so many feelings that black women must have—watching their beloved children grow up to be despised by some simply because of the color of their skin—and that he could never penetrate the feelings of a woman, or a mother as I might be able to do. He said that since he had written *Black Like Me* many women had come to him with the idea that they might try what he did.

"But I discouraged every one, because—until you—I never met anyone I thought could do it."

She read in *Esquire* magazine about Dr. Robert Stolar, a Washington, D.C., skin specialist who had turned many black men white. The article said, "it is easier for a white man to make himself black than for a black man to make himself white." Halsell doubted that Stolar ever tried that transition himself.

She made an appointment to see Stolar and told him what she wanted to do. He could give her a prescription she could get filled at any drugstore. "You might stay dark for a year," he said.

John Howard Griffin had to shave his head—his natural hair would have given him away as a white man; Grace Halsell got dark contact lenses; her blue eyes would have given away *her* secret.

She wanted a second medical opinion and consulted Dr. Aaron Lerner, at the Yale Medical Center. She told him she wanted to do what John Howard Griffin did—become black. And she asked him about drugs:

> What about the medication psoralen, I wanted to know.
>
> He told me the medical term was trimethyl psoralen, and said the label generally used is "trisoralen." Originally, he said, the medicine came from a plant in Egypt, but when it became difficult to secure, it was produced synthetically.
>
> He explained that skin color comes principally from the dark pigment melanin (produced

in cells known as melanocytes, sandwiched between outer and inner skin layers). The quality and distribution of melanin causes skin to be different colors in different parts of the body, and also plays the major role in the gradation of colors that is found from one individual to another.

The drug psoralen, taken orally before exposure to sunlight or ultraviolet light, steps up the melanin production process and turns light skin dark.

He gave her a prescription. "In two or three weeks you will be *very dark*," he said. And she bought a walnut stain, actually potassium permanganate, as a supplement.

Her skin dark, dark and contacts which turned her blue eyes black, Halsell journeyed to Harlem.

I've packed all of my own fears, right in with the nylons and hairbrush. I'm not supposed to go there .... The white man says the black man is a beast and marauder, he will rape you, rob you, he is mean as the devil (you know the devil has to be black). This mythology makes me a trespasser: I go where I have no "right" to be; my world won't condone it; my people wouldn't understand it.

* * *

I keep walking, clinging to the thought that there's always room for one more, always a room at the inn, just the right place is going to turn up. I pass the Black Panther headquarters, in an area where Harlem again presents a scene of despair and debasement; liquor stores, bars, and more liquid stores and bars. Churches, faith healers, beauty shops, small stores, small cares—no business you'd term "black business." And the people walking around imprisoned in an open-air jail, as if the place doesn't belong to them and they, too, are transient here.

* * *

It's not that the people are starving to death (my mind conjures up the thin sticks of bones strewn like debris, those dead and dying of India). And the people are not even *dirt* poor, like the poor of Paraguay, who live on the dirt and can extract edible roots from it. No, it is rather that here in Harlem they are reminded that they are the poorest of the poor in an affluent society because they have been denied their dreams and the American promise is a worthless lie.

John Howard Griffin saw the world through two venues—medicine and music. Halsell saw it through art:

I enter the Harlem Hospital emergency ward. A woman screams, and a nurse says it's a miscarriage. I see a man wheeled by on a stretcher, his head badly mangled.

I study the faces and am started by the agony and grief etched on them. This is precisely the way Goya and Daumier had painted the poor, the destitute, the forgotten people who have suffered beyond human capacity to endure, but somehow have gone on enduring as "faceless" women and men.

Obviously there are hundreds more patients than the emergency ward can handle. We are all reduced to the level of cogs arrayed for inspection on an assembly line. You're bleeding to death? Giving birth? Got an overdose? A broken leg? Shot in the groin? Stand here, move over, wait your turn, fill out this form, next group, please. Keep moving.

Now walk the streets with me, Halsell writes:

You see the old brownstones up close. Nearly all were built in a spurt of energy that lasted from the 1870s through the first decade of the twentieth century. You see streets littered with garbage, children chasing balls amid the cars; the drunks, the whores, the junkies, pushers, gamblers, pimps, the big ugly black scar on your white existence; you don't want to think, you look away. Now up close you see that those old brownstones that once wore the look of middle-class respectability now wear the neglect of corrupt, absentee ownership. The stoops are broken, covered with derelicts

and debris so thick it's like the excrement of the
guano birds, piles and piles of it.

Harlem was, she thought, much like a cemetery.
Those who were "in" don't feel they could get out and
those who were out don't want to be in.

Halsell traveled to New Orleans then picked Jackson,
Mississippi, and eventually got work as a "domestic," a
house maid for a mid-40s white woman:

> "First take a damp cloth and clean off all the
> clotheslines." When I return, she directs: "I want
> you to sweep down all the walls, all the ceilings,
> then use this other broom to clean all the rugs.
> Use the dust mop on all the floors, this rag for
> the living room furniture, and this rag for the
> dining room furniture. And move the furniture
> to sweep behind the sofa and chairs. Polish all
> the mirrors, and then go over the glass on the
> pictures and the glass on that china chest." And
> on and on.
>
> Long before I have one job completed there
> are new orders. "Now sweep off the front porch,
> the side porch, the back porch, and mop the
> back porch." (Her) tone is unmistakably that of
> the mistress-slave relationship.
>
> And, I am "working like a nigger," Halsell
> told herself.

Grace Halsell survived her black journey through
Harlem and the south without making the inadvertent

mistake that John Howard Griffin did, of moving back and forth between black and white worlds too quickly.

Before she began her odyssey into her black world, she told a black Washington, D.C. lawyer what she had planned and that she was going into the south. "You will go down there and get yourself killed," he told her. Ray Sprigle and John Howard Griffin surely heard those exact same words.

Soul Sister was published in hardcover in 1969 and in a paperback edition the next year. Grace Halsell later published nine additional books. She died in August 2000; her papers and archives are at Texas Christian University; with some at Boston University. Before her death, she willed that her author royalties should be given to Howard University, in Washington, D.C.. Like Virginia Union University, Howard is a historically black university. *Soul Sister* is now out-of-print, but hardcover and paperback copies are still available from used- and rare-book dealers.

Twelve

1991: Rodney King

"Can we all get along?"

SAVAGE ACTS OF POLICE brutality in California in March, 1991, videotaped by a bystander led to the costliest rioting in America, in terms of lives lost and property damage, and while the Bull Connor brutality images of the 1960s have largely faded into the past; the Rodney King videotape and riots remain etched in the American psyche.

Rodney King was born in Sacramento April 2, 1965; he grew up in Altadena, California. In November 1989, he robbed a store in Monterey Park, wielding an iron bar. He threatened a Korean store owner with the iron bar; he was caught, convicted and was sentenced to two years in prison. He was paroled after one year.

In the evening of March 2, 1991, he and two companions, Bryant Allen and Freddie Helms were driving west on the Foothill Freeway (Interstate 210) in the San Fernando Valley area of Los Angeles.

At 12;30 a.m. officers Tim and Melanie Singer, husband-and-wife team members of the California Highway Patrol, noticed King's car speeding. They pursued King, but he refused to pull over. King later stated that he refused to pull over because a charge of driving under the influence (of alcohol) would violate his parole for his earlier robbery conviction.

King left the Freeway and the high-speed pursuit continued. After about eight miles, officers cornered King in his car. The LAPD arrived—officers Stacey Koon, Laurence Powell, Timothy Wind, Theodore Briseno and Rolando Solano.

Officer Tim Singer ordered King and his passengers to leave the car—the two others, Allen and Helms did so and were arrested without incident. King got out, acted in a bizarre manner and waved to a police helicopter now hovering overhead. He grabbed for his buttocks, which officer Melanie Singer believed to mean he was reaching for a weapon. She drew her weapon and approached him, preparing to arrest him.

At this point, Stacy Koon, the ranking member of the LAPD announced that the LAPD would be in charge. He ordered the other LAPD officers to holster their weapons; LAPD officers are instructed not to approach a suspect with weapons drawn, as a suspect may attempt to grab an officer's weapon. Koon then ordered the LAPD officers to "swarm" King. King was able to throw officers Powell and Briseno off his back; LAPD officers then believed that King had taken the drug phencyclidine (PCP) although a toxicology test later proved negative for that drug.

King was hit by high-voltage Tasar weapons *twice* and overcame both electric charges.

At this point, George Holliday watching from nearby, began videotaping the incident.

King is shown on the tape rising, and moving to attack officer Powell or to escape. King and Powell collide; Powell hits King with his baton and King falls to the ground. Powell hits him several more times; Briseno moves in attempting to stop Powell from hitting King again. Koon apparently says "that's enough," but Powell and Wind are seen on the tape, continuing to hit King.

Koon then ordered the continuing use of the batons—ordering Powell and Wind to hit King with "power strokes."

Koon ordered the officers to "hit his joints, hit his wrists, hit his elbows, hit his knees, hit his ankles."

Holliday continued videotaping the assault.

The officers miss occasionally, but hit King 33 blows, plus six kicks. They again "swarm" him, this time with eight officers, and finally subdue his arms and legs. King is dragged on his stomach to the side of the road to await the arrival of an EMS van.

Two days later George Holiday told the LAPD about his videotape and then took it to Los Angeles television station KTLA, which broadcast it immediately.

The tape was broadcast again and again, over and over and over and over. And nationally again and again, over and over. And internationally again and again, over and over.

It became an early example of "people power"—individuals with video cams and now cellphones, who can record and transmit events as they are happening. And with video cams and cellphones, citizens can now disprove fraudulent, self-serving, contradictory statements or out-right lies by officials.

King was taken to Pacifica Hospital. When he was examined he had suffered a fractured facial bone, a broken right ankle and multiple bruises and lacerations. King sued the City of Los Angeles and claimed he suffered "11 skull fractures, permanent brain damage, broken (bones and teeth), kidney damage and emotional and physical stress." Tests indicated he was intoxicated under California law. The tests also showed a minor amount of marijuana in his system, but nothing else.

Pacifica nurses reported that officers who took King to the hospital bragged about the number of times King had been hit.

A jury awarded him $3.8 million and an additional $1.7 million in legal fees.

The Los Angeles District Attorney charged officers Koon, Powell, Briseno and Wind with use of excessive force. Koon had not hit King, but had used a Tasar. The trial was moved out of Los Angeles to Simi Valley, a largely white enclave-suburb of Los Angeles, where some LAPD officers lived. The jury consisted of nine white members, one black, one Latino and one Asian.

Despite the Holliday tape, which Los Angeles television continued to replay, on April 29, 1992, the jury *acquitted all four* officers of assault and could not agree on an excessive force charge against Powell.

Rioting began the same day as the Simi Valley verdicts.

The verdict was announced at 3:15 p.m. By 3:45 more than 300 protestors had gathered at the Los Angeles County Courthouse building. Others gathered at the intersection of Florence and Normandie in south central Los Angeles. More appeared at the Police Department headquarters at Parker Center.

They were quickly named the Rodney King Riots and also, the South Central Riots.

On the second day, April 30, violence, looting and destruction was apparent through Los Angeles County. There were open gun battles in the Koreatown area, between shop owners and looters. Fire crews began being escorted by police; California Highway Patrol units were airlifted to the city. The California National Guard loaned equipment to other law enforcement units and 2,000 members of the National Guard were called into service, but were delayed for 24 hours by a lack of equipment and available ammunition.

On the third day, May 1, Rodney King made an appearance in front of his lawyer's office. "People, I just want to say, you know, can we all get along?" The "Can we all get along?" statement was allegedly supplied by his attorney; King was apparently too inarticulate to ad-lib even a short speech.

National Guard troops were doubled to 4,000 and eventually to 10,000. A variety of 1,700 federal law-enforcement officers from different agencies began to arrive to protect federal facilities. President George H.W. Bush addressed the nation, condemning "random terror and lawlessness." He ordered the Justice Department to review the case. Professional games involving the Los Angeles Lakers and the L.A. Clippers were postponed. The baseball Dodgers also postponed games. A curfew in San Francisco caused a game with the San Francisco Giants and the Phillies to be postponed. Horse racing was not held; a Van Halen concert was cancelled. Bus service halted. Some freeways closed. The World Wrestling Federation cancelled events in Long Beach and Fresno.

On the fourth day (Saturday, May 2), 2,000 members of the 7th Infantry Division, from Fort Ord arrived, as did 1,500 Marines from Camp Pendleton. A total of 13,500 U.S. military forces were then helping support law enforcement. The Justice Department announced it would begin an investigation.

On the fifth day, Sunday, 3 and the sixth day, Monday, May 4, rioting and looting ceased. Schools, business and stores reopened on Monday, but federal troops did not stand down until May 14 and some stayed deployed until May 26.

The sum total: 53 died during the riots, including 10 who were shot dead by police or military forces; over 2,383 were injured. The total estimates in property damage ranged from $800 million to $1 billion. There were more than 7,000 fires. 3,767 buildings were set on fire. Korean and Asian immigrants seemed to be widely targeted. Some buildings were never rebuilt. Half of those arrested and more than half killed were Hispanic.

Although the Rodney King videotape and the not guilty verdicts seemed to be the tipping point, later analysis pointed to high unemployment in minority communities, poor housing, conflicts between the black population and the Hispanic population of Los Angeles, and other sociological problems as contributing factors.

There were also riots in San Francisco; Las Vegas; Atlanta and even as far away as Toronto, Canada.

A t-shirt was sold throughout Los Angeles: on the front it read LAPD with a large LAPD logo. On the back it read: THEY TREAT YOU LIKE A KING.

Weeks after the rioting, 11,000 people continued to be arrested.

After the riots, extensive and prolonged civic debate began, at the local, state and national level.

The Justice Department did, as promised, re-open the case; and filed federal civil rights charges against LAPD officers Stacey Koon, Lawrence Powell, Timothy Wind and Theodore Briseno. Rodney King testified in the case. Koon and Powell were found guilty and sentenced to 32 months in prison; Wind and Briseno were acquitted of all charges. None returned to the LAPD.

In the article "Rodney King and MLK" in the book *Inside the L.A. Riots: What Really Happened—and Why It Will Happen Again*," Harvey Wasserman wrote:

> Nearly a quarter century—within a year and few days—passed between the murder of Martin Luther King and the acquittal of the cops who beat Rodney King.
>
> What progress has been made in the interim?

The inner-cities ravaged in the uprising following the King murder were never rebuilt by the time of the King verdict.

We have traded Thurgood Marshall for Clarence Thomas. Lyndon Johnson for George Bush.

* * *

In a quarter-century what lessons have been learned from the death of Martin Luther King? His leadership has never been replaced. The lethal uprisings that followed his murder helped no one, translated into no positive action, raised no conscience or lasting consciousness among the nation's decision-makers. What came instead was a deep-seated neighborhood hopelessness, fought off with great difficulty by community organizers, but exploited ever since by the likes of Nixon, Reagan and Bush.

* * *

And it is easy to forget that, for nonviolence to ultimately work, it requires a civilized response from those in power.

Twenty-four years after the loss of our greatest preacher of non-violent direct action, do we see any evidence of that moral or mental capacity in our government?

And, if not, what right do we have to be surprised when the torches and bullets once again fly, deadlier than ever?

A statistic accompanying that article revealed:

Average home price, Los Angeles, 1990:
$224,000.
Average home price, South Central L.A., 1990:
$127,000.

Rodney King had drug problems before and after the famous police beating video. On June 17, 2012, King's fiancee Cynthia Kelly found him at the bottom of his swimming pool. He was pronounced dead at a Colton, California, hospital. An autopsy found alcohol, marijuana, cocaine and the drug PCP in his system. The cause of death was classified as accidental drowning, with the autopsy findings listed as contributing factors in his death.

Rodney King was 47.

Thirteen |

1998: James Byrd, Jr.

Murdered in Jasper, Texas, June 7, 1998
Age: 49

JASPER, TEXAS, IS APPROXIMATELY 135 miles northeast of Houston. Driving up Route 69, 30 miles from Houston toward Jasper, is New Caney, Texas. After the Civil War, Confederate veterans disappeared into the woods in the New Caney area and never came out. Even in the early and mid-1990s, utility crews were *very* reluctant to service accounts in the New Caney area. *Very reluctant to stop in New Caney.*

Driving on, 100 miles-plus northeast, up the same highway from New Caney, is Jasper, Texas, in an area known as The Big Thicket, rich in wildlife. It shares the same history.

As Dina Temple-Raston writes, in *A Death in Texas*:

> Deep east Texas has always been insular,
> and the attitude was rooted in history. When the

Louisiana Purchase failed to clearly designate the new western boundary of the United States in 1803, the United States and Spain agreed the swath of land along the Sabine River—the current Texas-Louisiana state line—would be neutral ground. Until the official boundary could be determined, both countries agreed not to enforce their laws there. The area became a no-man's land, a safe haven for murderers, rapists, thieves, and fugitives from authority. Most Texans said East Texas wasn't really Texas. Residents behind "the pine curtain" had failed to come out of the woods during the great westward movement. They were, people in Houston said, different.

Nearly two hundred years later, not much has changed—partly because Jasperites were so concerned with just getting by. Events that occurred in Houston, Birmingham, and New York occurred in a world far removed from the piney woods and double-wide trailers of Jasper. The town's residents watched the civil rights marches in Birmingham on their television sets and drew away from the violence hoping that the black national storm would somehow blow itself out before it reached the edge of their woods. And when the time came, and the law required the whites to allow the blacks to come in the front door, Jasper did just that.

In 1954, *Brown v. the Board of Education* fell on Jasper like a fist. After three centuries of black oppression, the Supreme Court of the United States had decided, on May 17, 1954, that African-Americans were entitled to everything whites already had. Blacks had to be treated as equals everywhere, beginning in the public schools. Overnight, segregation in the schools was decreed unconstitutional and against the law.

In the white south there was gloom and in Jasper there was disbelief.

It took fourteen years to integrate. There was some wiggle room in the Court's decision and Jasper's white community didn't want to rush things, because, frankly, they were worried about whether everyone would get along just because the Supreme Court said they must.

"Negroes" was the word whites used in polite company then; "black" was the word they used in public in the 1990s. Behind closed doors, however, "nigger" was part of the vernacular, used both as a noun and an adjective. As a noun, to describe an individual in the black community, it usually had an adjective added to it: "good nigger," "fucking nigger," or "poor nigger."

On June 7, 1998, James Byrd, Jr., 49, of Jasper, was drinking with friends. "You watch," he said, "when I go, everyone is going to call me Mr. Byrd."

Just hours later, he accepted a ride from John King, 23, Lawrence Russell Brewer, 31, and Shawn Berry, 24. Berry knew Byrd from Jasper. Instead of taking Byrd home, as promised, they drove around Jasper, then took him to a remote part of the country, beat him, urinated on him, and chained him by the ankles to their pickup truck. They then dragged Byrd behind the truck for three miles. The truck even swerved side to side to bounce him across the road. Byrd attempted to keep his head up while being dragged and attempted to support himself on his arms and elbows, but his arms were sheared to the bone; he was apparently conscious during much of the ordeal.

He died when his body hit a culvert; his head and his right arm were severed.

King, Brewer and Berry dumped Byrd's mangled body then went to a local barbeque.

King and Brewer had been in the Texas prison system, in the Beto unit, in 1995, which was considered a "gladiator" unit, with 3,000 inmates. King had white racist tattoos, including one of a hanging black man and a shield on his side with the words ARYAN PRIDE. Berry had been in trouble with the police, but had avoided prison.

The next day, investigators found a wrench with the word "Berry" on it and a lighter with KKK on one side and *Possum* on the other, King's prison nickname. Brewer had become a member of the Klu Klux Klan in prison.

Investigators found Byrd's head and arm then, and 81 places that were littered with Bryd's remains.

Since Brewer and King were widely known as white supremacists, the FBI was called in, less than 24 hours after Bryd was killed, and the crime was officially declared a hate crime.

All three were tried separately; Brewer and King were condemned to death; but Berry, who also was a racist, apparently was the least involved in the murder, and was sentenced to life in prison.

Doug Miller, of Houston television station KHOU, interviewed Brewer in prison for an article which was posted on the KHOU website September 20, 2011.

"As far as regrets, no, I have no regrets," Brewer says, "No, I'd do it over again, to tell you the truth."

Billy Rowles, then retired sheriff, who investigated the murders, said of Brewer, "In all the time he sat in that cement cage, that he's been in there, in all the time that he's had to think, I cannot believe there's not some kind of remorse."

Byrd's murder, and the national outcry that ensued, again highlighted racism in America. Basketball star Dennis Rodman paid for Byrd's funeral expenses and gave Byrd's family $25,000. Boxing promoter Don King gave Byrd's children $100,000., for their college educations.

In Texas, the 77th Legislature passed the James Byrd, Jr. Hate Crimes Act.

Three months later that year, Matthew Shepard was killed in Wyoming. He was 21, a student at the University of Wyoming and gay; his body was found strung on a fence line outside Laramie, October 12, 1998. The official course of death was homicide, but he had been tortured and left to die, apparently solely because he was gay.

In October, 2009, the U.S. Congress passed the Matthew Shepard and James Byrd, Jr. Hate Crimes Prevention Act, now commonly known as the Matthew

Shepard Act. On October 28, 2009, President Barack Obama signed it into law.

After the national attention to the 1998 hate crime killing of James Byrd, Jr., do you think that members of the Jasper, Texas, community would have changed their outlook on racial equality?

Think carefully. Then think again.

As an example, the Jasper local cemetery, which is privately owned, is on a hillside.

An article, "Racial Tensions Flare Anew in a Texas Town," by Manny Fernandez, appeared in *The New York Times* June 21, 2012. Fernandez describes how Jasper continues to be split racially:

> JASPER, Tx.—For more than 100 years, a rickety iron fence separated the black graves from the one ones at a cemetery in this East Texas town. Months after the brutal murder here of James Byrd, Jr., a black man chained to a pickup truck and dragged to his death by three white men on June 7, 1998, the fence was torn down by residents as a sign of unity and reconciliation.
>
> Fourteen years later, Jasper City Cemetery remains segregated: blacks, including Mr. Byrd, are buried near the bottom of the hill, while whites are buried at the top.
>
> "It's our custom, here in the South, here in Jasper," said Albert K. Snell, 80, a retired teacher who is white and a members of the cemetery's board of directors. "We have the same cemetery,

but we don't mix the white and the black graves. They're separate. Put a black up here? No, no, we wouldn't do that. That would be against our custom, against our way of doing things."

In 2004, two white teenagers desecrated the James Byrd, Jr. gravesite with spray-painted racial slurs and knocked over his headstone.

In 2011, the Jasper City Council had a majority of black members. They voted to hire Rodney Pearson, to be Jasper's first black police chief. Pearson was a former Texas State Trooper (Texas highway patrolman) and was the first police officer on the scene when James Byrd's body was found.

The act of appointing a black police chief led to a prolonged and nasty *contretemps*; outraged white citizens of Jasper forced a referendum and voted out the majority of black City Council members. With a white majority then in the City Council, Rodney Pearson was fired. His wife Sandy, who is white and had nothing whatsoever to do with the politics in Jasper, lost her job as an office manager. The fighting was bitter; Pearson brought in the Texas NAACP and asked the federal government to investigate. White citizens also filed discrimination lawsuits.

Newly-elected white members of the City Council said that Pearson was forced out lacked sufficient qualifications for the office of Jasper Police Chief.

Alton Scott, one of the (former) black City Council members said, "The whole thing is racist. It's based on race. It has nothing to do with Pearson's qualifications."

At the time of the Pearson controversy in 2011, Jasper was 45 percent white and 44 percent black.

The wrought-iron cemetery fence, torn down in a show of unity, was eventually replaced by another fence, separating the white and black areas of the Jasper cemetery.

Fourteen |

2012: Treyvon Martin

"We don't need you to do that."

Sunday, February 26, 2012,
approximately 7 p.m., Sanford, Florida
Dispatcher: Sanford Police Department

(GEORGE) ZIMMERMAN: HEY, WE'VE had some break-ins in my neighborhood, and there's a real suspicious guy, uh (near) Retreat View Circle, um, the best address I can give you is 111 Retreat View Circle. The guy looks like he's up to no good, or he's on drugs or something. It's raining and he's just walking around, looking about ...

Dispatcher: OK, and this guy, is he white, black, or hispanic?

Zimmerman: He looks black.

Dispatcher: Did you see what he is wearing?

Zimmerman: Yeah. A dark hoodie, like a grey hoodie, and either jeans or sweatpants and white tennis shoes. He's (unintelligible), he was just staring ...

Dispatcher: OK, he's just walking around the area ...

Zimmerman: ... looking at all the houses.

Dispatcher: OK.

Zimmerman, Now he's just staring at me.

Dispatcher: OK—you said it's 1111 Retreat View? Or 111?

Zimmerman: Thats the clubhouse ...

Dispatcher: That's the clubhouse, do you know what the—he's near the clubhouse right now?

Zimmerman: Yeah, now he's coming towards me.

Dispatcher: OK.

Zimmerman: He's got his hand in his waistband, And he's a black male.

Dispatcher: How old would you say he looks?

Zimmerman: He's got a button on his shirt. Late teens.

Dispatcher: Late teens OK.

Simmerman: Something's wrong with him. Yup, he's coming to check me out, he's got something in his hands. Don't know what his deal is.

Dispatcher: Just let me know if he does anything, OK.

Zimmerman: How long until you get an officer over here?

Dispatcher: Yeah, we've got someone on the way, just let me know if this guy does anything else.

Zimmerman: OK. These assholes—they always get away. When you come to the clubhouse you come straight in and make a left. Actually you go past the clubhouse.

Dispatcher: So it's on the left side from the Clubhouse?

Zimmerman: No you go in straight through the entrance and then you make a left ... uh you go straight in, don't turn, and make a left. Shit, he's running.

Dispatcher: He's running? Which way is he running?

Zimmerman: Down toward the other entrance to the neighborhood.

Dispatcher: Which entrance is that that he's heading towards?

Zimmerman: The back entrance ... fucking (unintelligible).

Dispatcher: Are you following him?

Zimmerman: Yeah.

Dispatcher: We don't need you to do that.

Zimmerman: OK.

Dispatcher: Alright sir, what is your name?

Zimmerman: George ... He ran.

Dispatcher: Alright George, what is your last name?

Zimmerman: Zimmerman.

Dispatcher: And George, what's the phone number you're calling from?

Zimmerman: (redacted).

Dispatcher: Alright George, we do have them on the way. Do you want to meet with the officer when they get there?

Zimmerman: Alright, where are you going to meet with them at?

Zimmerman: If they come straight through the gate, tell them to go straight past the clubhouse, and uh, straight past the clubhouse and make a left, and then they go past the mailboxes, that's my truck (unintelligible).

Dispatcher: What address are you parked in front of?

Zimmerman; I don't know, it's a cut through so I don't know the address.

Dispatcher: OK, do you live in the area?

Zimmerman: Yeah, I ... (unintelligible)

Dispatcher: What's your apartment number?

Zimmerman: It's a home it's 1950, oh crap I don't want to give it all out. I don't know where this kid is.

Dispatcher: Ok, do you want to just meet with them right near the mailboxes then?

Zimmerman: Yeah, that's fine.

Dispatcher: Alright George, I'll let them know to meet you there, OK?

Zimmerman: Actually could you have them call me and I'll tell them where I'm at?

Dispatcher: OK, yeah, that's no problem.

Zimmerman: Should I give you my number or you got it?

Dispatcher: Yeah I got it. (redacted)

Zimmerman: Yeah, you got it.

Dispatcher: OK, no problem, I'll let them know
    to call you when you're in the area.

Zimmerman: Thanks.

Dispatcher: You're welcome.

And so it began.

George Zimmerman was 28; his father white, his mother, hispanic, from Peru. Treyvon Martin, 17, was black.

Zimmerman wanted to be a police officer or a judge and was majoring in Criminal Justice at a local community college, but he had been in trouble with the police before. He had been accused of domestic violence by a former girlfriend and had been previously arrested for assaulting a police officer. A cousin of Zimmerman's accused him of years of sexual molestation and she also accused members of Zimmerman's family of being proudly racist against African Americans and she recalled examples of perceived bigotry.

At the time of the confrontation with Treyvon Martin, Zimmerman was a neighborhood watch coordinator for the gated community where Martin was temporarily staying.

From a police report later, Treyvon Martin was doing nothing suspicious or illegal, at the time. *He was just walking home.* He was returning home from a store with a bag of Skittles and ice tea. From Zimmerman's perspective, the hoodie and Martin's "behavior" made him a suspect; many believe that is pure racial profiling.

Zimmerman left his truck and confronted Martin. There was a argument—a struggle—a violent encounter.

Zimmerman sustained cuts on the back of his head, so inconsequential they needed no stitches; he also suffered a bleeding, or perhaps, a broken nose.

Later, during his trial, tapes were played of their encounter; screams could be heard on the tape. Martin's mother claimed the screams were Trayvon's; Zimmerman's mother claimed the screams were Zimmerman. A shot could be heard on the tape, then the screaming stopped. Most would believe the screams were Treyvon Martin, who stopped screaming when he was shot. Shot by Zimmerman. Trayvon Martin was shot at extremely close range and died almost immediately.

When police arrived, they found that Zimmerman had used a 9 mm handgun. (His "firearm," he said later, in police jargon.) He claimed he shot Martin in self-defense.

He was taken to the Sanford Police headquarters, questioned for approximately five hours and released. At the time, Police found nothing that would contradict his claim of self-defense.

The initial decision not to charge Zimmerman caused national outrage, a consequence of "Stand Your Ground" laws passed in Florida and elsewhere. (The Sanford Police Chief later resigned or was forced to resign for the lack of an immediate arrest.)

From earliest Anglo-Saxon laws, "a man's home is his castle," and homeowners are quite within their rights to shoot intruders. "Stand Your Ground" laws made it acceptable to allow deadly force *anywhere*.

They allow people who believe they are imminently threatened to use deadly force *before* retreating from the threat. Cynics have called them "Make My Day"

laws from the "Dirty Harry"/Clint Eastwood charac-
ter: *Go ahead and do something and I'll shoot you ... go
ahead—Make My Day* ....

"Stand Your Ground" laws were first promulgated
by the American Legislative Exchange Council (ALEC),
a largely-right wing organization, in concert with the
National Rifle Association. Their plan was to introduce
"Stand Your Ground" legislation to "red" (Republican-
controlled) states, then eventually roll out that concept
throughout the country.

The history of adoptions of "Stand Your Ground"
laws is:

1900s	Connecticut, Hawaii, Iowa, Utah.
2004	Illinois.
2005	Florida, Nevada.
2005	Alabama, Alaska, Arizona, Georgia, Idaho, Indiana, Kansas, Kentucky, Louisiana, Michigan, Mississippi. Oklahoma, South Carolina, South Dakota.
2007	Missouri, North Dakota, Tennessee, Texas, Wisconsin.
2008	Ohio, West Virginia, Wyoming.
2011	New Hampshire, North Carolina, Pennsylvania.

However, during the Zimmerman trial, "Stand Your
Ground" became part of the national dialogue; and,
perhaps as a surprise to ALEC, nearly 30 major U.S.
corporations dropped their membership in ALEC. They

included: Kraft Foods; Pepsico; Coca-Cola; Hewlett-Packard; CVS Caremark; Deere and Co; MillerCoors; BestBuy; Dell Computer; Amazon; Intuit; Medtronic and others. Their corporate resignations were obviously based on two logical points: "Stand Your Ground" laws had no bearing on the corporate objectives of these companies and, secondly, none wanted the negative publicity associated with ALEC. The National Rifle Association, however, stood—and still stands—resolutely with ALEC.

After the death of Trayvon Martin, President Obama said, "If I had a son, he would be Trayvon."

On March 22, 2012, a Special Prosecutor was appointed to take over the case; on April 11, 2012 a charge of murder in the second degree was filed against George Zimmerman.

Zimmerman's trial was begun in Sanford, Florida, June 10, 2013. He had requested a "Stand Your Ground" hearing, but his defense attorneys elected to bypass that hearing so his case would be tried before a jury.

The Zimmerman jury was all female; they had three choices; Murder in the Second Degree, Manslaughter, or Acquittal. When the jury was dismissed to deliberate Zimmerman's fate, Judge Debra Nelson instructed the jurors in the "Stand Your Ground" rationale:

> *If George Zimmerman was not engaged in an unlawful activity and was attacked in any place where he had a right to be, he had no duty to retreat and had the right to stand his ground and meet force with force.*

Presumably the jury also remembered that Zimmerman had followed Treyvon Martin even after the Police Dispatcher told him "we don't need you to do that," and they presumably remembered the idea of racial profiling, when Zimmerman said, on the Dispatcher's tape, "These assholes—they always get away."

After deliberating 16 hours, the jury found Zimmerman *Not Guilty* in the death of Treyvon Martin.

The verdict has again taken over the national dialogue on race and justice. There have been demonstrations in major cities against the verdict, but they have been, fortunately, for the most part, peaceful. Print publications, television, radio, cable, and commentators on all sides of the political spectrum have contributed to the dialogue.

Trayvon Martin has become the Emmett Till of this century.

Artist Nikkolas Smith has contributed a remarkable image, a picture of a dark hoodie, like Trayvon Martin wore, *with the face of Martin Luther King, Jr.* That image has rocketed back and forth throughout the internet.

What can we say about Florida Governor Rick Scott, who took the "Stand Your Ground" proposed laws and marched them through the Republican-controlled Florida state legislature ... then presented them to the Florida public as a *fait accompli* ... ? Doing the bidding of ALEC and the National Rifle Association ... ? We can think of Bob Dylan's song about Byron De La Beckwith:

He's only a pawn in their game.

On Friday, July 19, 2013, President Barack Obama entered the press room of the White House, unexpectedly, and, in a remarkably personal and candid statement, said:

"When Trayvon Martin was first shot, I said that this could have been my son. Another way of saying that is, Treyvon Martin could have been me, 35 years ago."

* * *

And finally ... in early August, 2013, Lonnie Bunch, Director of the National Museum of African-American History and Culture, a division of the Smithsonian, in Washington, D.C.—the nation's museum—has said he would like to acquire the hoodie worn by Trayvon Martin, when he was killed by George Zimmerman.

The new National Museum of African-American History and Culture is set to open in 2015.

"It became the symbolic way to talk about the Trayvon Martin case," Bunch told *The Washington Post*. "It's rare that you get one artifact that really became the symbol.

"Because it's such a symbol, it would allow you to talk about race in the age of Obama."

Epilogue ...

IT HAS NOW BEEN 50 years since Martin Luther King, Jr. gave his "I Have a Dream Speech," in Washington, D.C., August 23, 1963.

Much progress has been made during these years ... ... and yet ... and yet ...

In his essay, "Race in America: A More Perfect Union?" published in *The Huffington Post*, on the internet, July 23, 2013, after the Treyvon Martin verdict, University of Chicago Law Professor Geoffrey R. Stone wrote:

1) Black Americas are twice as likely as white Americans to live in poverty.

2) Black Americans are twice as likely as white Americans to be unemployed.

3) The median family income of black Americans is only 67 percent of that of white Americans.

4) The average white American family's net worth is 22 times greater than that of the average black American family.

5) The average white American family is 58 percent more likely to own a home than the average black family.

6) Black American eighth graders are almost three times more likely to read below basic reading levels than white American eight graders.

7) Black American students are more than twice as likely to drop out of high school than white American students.

8) Black American college students are 42 percent less likely to graduate college in four years than white American college students.

9) Black American males are six times more likely to be incarcerated than white American males.

10) Black American criminal defendants are sentenced to death three times more often than white American defendants when the victim was white.

11) Black American criminal defendants are sentenced to 10 percent longer prison terms than white American criminal defendants for the same crime.

12) Black American drivers are three times more likely to be searched when they are stopped for a traffic violation than white American drivers.

13) A white American is four times more likely to become a lawyer than a black American.

14) A white American is three times more likely to become a doctor than a black American.

15) The United States Senate includes 98 white Americans and black Americans.

16) White Americans are almost twice as likely as black Americans to think that black Americans have made significant progress in recent years.

Stone also wrote:

And in the face of all this, the conservative justices of the United States Supreme Court insist that affirmative action programs designed to provide black Americans with some semblance of equal opportunity in higher education and the Voting Rights Act of 1965 are both unconstitutional because we have, after all, made progress.

During the last week in July, 2013, some residents in Springfield, Missouri, woke up to find the Klu Klux Klan had distributed flyers throughout their neighborhood.

In an article headlined, "Ku Klux Klan Neighborhood Watch Program: Group Offers to Handle Neighbors' 'Troubles'" in *The Christian Post*, July 26, 2013, reporter Brittany R. Villalva wrote:

The Klu Klux Klan has begun initiatives to start programs across the nation.

The groups' decision to start a neighborhood watch program comes less than a month after neighborhood watchman George Zimmerman was found "not guilty" of murdering Trayvon Martin. Early efforts to recruit members for a watch program began in Springfield, Mo., where local residents received flyers from the Traditionalist American Knights of the Klu Klux Klan.

The flyers depict a man wearing a traditional Klan hood and logo, pointing a finger. The flyer promotes a "neighborhood watch" program with the phrase: "You can sleep tonight knowing the Klan is awake." Below the quote a number is provided encouraged (sic) those with "troubles" in the neighborhood to contact the Klan.

And so, the struggle for social justice continues ...

Notes on Sources

Chapter 1

Page

1   "All right, then, I'll go to hell ..." Twain, *Adventures of Huckleberry Finn*. New York: Book of the Month Club edition, 1992, pp. 297.

2   "He never left Hannibal ..." James Thurber, America's 20th century Mark Twain, never left Columbus, Ohio, his birthplace; he wrote about it—and its varied citizens—throughout his life.

3   "The old gentleman was not ..." Twain, *Life on the Mississippi*. New York: Book of the Month Club edition, 1992, pp. 401.

5   "Thus Mark Twain was born." The four most famous pseudonyms in literature are: Charles Lutwidge Dodgson "Lewis Carroll"; "Mark Twain"; Theodor "Dr. Seuss" Geisel and "George Orwell," Eric Blair.

6   "Beneath the whites were the blacks." Lauber, *The Making of Mark Twain*, pp. 24.

8   "In this book ..." Twain, *Adventures of Huckleberry Finn*, no pagination.

10   "At last I had an idea." *Ibid.*, pp. 295.

12   "When he wrote ..." Noble, *Bookbanning in America*, pp. 268.

13   In 1885, *Ibid.*, pp. 209

14   "In time *Huckleberry Finn* ..." Kaplan, *Mr. Clemens and Mark Twain*, pp. 267.

Chapter 2

Page

17   ... university parking lot ..." After substantial civic protests, Virginia Commonwealth University, a state university, abandoned plans for a parking lot on the Lumpkin's Jail historic site.

15, 21 "The classroom windows ..." Hylton, "About VUU—History," Virginia Union University website: www.VUU.edu.

Chapter 3

Page

24   "Sprigle's name was not exactly unknown ..." Fensch, *The Man Who Changed His Skin*, pp. 61.

26   "I was a Negro in the Deep South." Sprigle, *In the Land of Jim Crow*, pp. 1

35   "She is worn and aged and bent beyond her time." *Ibid.* pp. 43.

Chapter 4

Page

42   "Little Mississippi." Emmett Till entry, Wikipedia. www.Wikipedia.com

42   "In the 1940s ..." Whitfield, *A Death in the Delta*, pp. 15.

43   "Mississippi was the poorest state ..." Emmett Till entry, Wikipedia.

43   "... it was a terrible ..." Whitfield, *A Death in the Delta*, pp. 117.

44   "His mother ... warned him ..." Wikipedia.

45   "The town had ..." Whitfield, *A Death in the Delta*, pp. 16.

46   Wright also explained ... *Ibid.*, pp. 18.

46   "Milam was thirty-six ..." *Ibid.*, pp. 20.

47   "he called them bastards..,." Till entry, Wikipedpia.

47   "What else could we do?" Huie, "The Shocking Story of Approved Killing in Mississippi," *Look* magazine, Jan. 1956.

48   "Accused of stealing ..." Till Wikipedia entry.

48   "They drove to a gin ..." Whitfield, *A Death in the Delta*, pp. 21.

49   "Soon the Mississippi field secretary ..." Till Wikipedia entry

49   "Till's swollen and disfigured ..." *Ibid.*

49   "so mangled and decomposed ..." *A Death in the Delta*, pp. 22

49   "the beating ..." *Ibid*, pp. 22.

50   "The A.A. Rayner ..." Till Wikipedia entry.

50   "Have you ever ..." Brinkley, pp. 101.

51   "none of the 19,000 ..." Whitfield, *A Death in the Delta*, pp. 82. (Italics added.)

51   Halberstam, "the first great media event ..." quoted in Till Wikipedia entry.

51   "Sheriff Strider ..." *Ibid.*

52   "The jury came back in 67 minutes ..." *Ibid.*

52   *Le Figaro* ..." Whitfield, *A Death in the Delta*, pp. 46.

53   "Huie interviews with Bryant and Milam, *Ibid.* pp. 52.

53   "I am not a liberal ..." *Ibid.*, pp. 53.

54   Till memorials, Wikipedia.

56   writers, poets, musicians, Wikipedia and *Death in the Delta*, pp. 65, 99.

57   Cook County autopsy, Wikipedia.

57   Deaths of Bryant and Milam, Wikipedia.

57   Willie Louis testimony, "Willie Louis, Who Named the Killers of Emmett Till at Their Trial, Dies at 76," Margalit Fox, *The New York Times*, July 24, 2013.

Chapter 5

Page

59   "Y'all better ...," bus confrontation, Parks Wikipedia entry.

60   "People always say ..." *Rosa Parks: My Story*, pp. 116.

60   Strictly speaking *Rosa Parks: My Story* not an adult autobiography; it is considered a YA book, a Young Adult book, written for pre-teens and teenagers.

61   "Somewhere in the machinery ..." Cleaver, quoted in *Rosa Parks: A Life*, Brinkley, pp. 2.

61   "A Rosa Parks moment ..." *Ibid.*, pp. 4.

61   "A plywood shanty ..." *Ibid*, pp. 11.

62   Farmer, quoted in Brinkley, pp. 6.

62   "Often ill ..." *Ibid*., pp. 14.

63   Mulatto ... *Ibid*., pp. 62.

63   Origins of Jim Crow, and "Beginning around 1875 ..." *Ibid*., pp. 31.

63   Colin Powell, quoted in Brinkley, pp. 31.

64   "There was a little table," Parks, *Rosa Parks: My Story*, pp. 67.

65   First confrontation with Blake, Montgomery bus driver, Brinkley, pp. 58.

66   "cup of endurance ..." King, *Stride Toward Freedom*, pp. 44.

66   Claudette Colvin, Brinkley, pp. 87.

67   Highlander Folk School, *Ibid*., pp. 91.

67   "When I made that decision ..." and "And her formal dignified 'No,'" ... *Ibid*., pp. 107.

68   "Soldiers who gave Christ vinegar ...," *Ibid*., pp. 110.

69   3,500 flyers, *Ibid*., pp. 123.

69   35,000 flyers, *The Autobiography of Medgar Evers*, pp. xix.

70   Nixon, "You ministers have lived ..." quoted in Brinkley, pp. 133.

70 King, "I'm not a coward ..." quoted in Brinkley, pp. 133.

71 King, "Since it had to happen ..." quoted in Brinkley, pp. 139.

73 King death threat, in Brinkley, pp. 149.

73 "Martin Luther ..." King, quoted in Brinkley, pp. 150.

74 Nixon bomb, Brinkley, pp. 153.

75 "My symbol shot ..." Parks quoted in Brinkley, pp. 171.

76 "When Parks was arrested ..." *Ibid.*, pp. 208.

77 "The first march ..." "Selma to Montgomery marches," Wikipedia.

77 "In the north in 1968 ..." Brinkley, pp. 208.

78 Awards, honors, Wikipedia.

Chapter 6

Page

83 "If I returned ..." (chapter sub-head), Griffin, *Black Like Me*, Signet ed., pp. 11.

84 "I worked in France ..." Griffin quoted in Fensch, *The Man Who Changed His Skin*, pp. 3.

85   Gestapo death lists, *Ibid.*, pp. 4.

85   "Witnessed the tragic effects ..." Bonazzi, in Fensch, pp. 5.

86   Parts of his tribal phonetic translations appear in Fensch, pp. 15.

87   "The black edge of a ravine," Griffin, in Fensch, pp. 26.

87   Been in the army for more than four years ... Fensch, pp. 27.

87   "I was stupefied ..." Griffin in Fensch, pp. 28.

88   "We continued through ..." Griffin, in Fensch, pp. 28.

89   "I feared myself ..." Griffin In Fensch, pp. 29.

91   Newspaper headlines, in Fensch, pp. 42. The headlines are in the Griffin archives, at Columbia University: however, the newspaper names have been clipped off; presumably they are all Texas newspapers.

92   "I learned to type ..." Griffin in Fensch, pp. 43.

93   "I had always been ..." Griffin in Fensch, pp. 44.

93   "Redness swirled in front ..." Griffin, in Fensch, pp. 49.

94   Newspaper headlines, Fensch, pp. 53.

95   "I could have been ..." Bonazzi, *Man in the Mirror*, pp. 171.

96   "Now you go into oblivion." *Black Like Me*, Signet ed., pp. 9.

97   "I stood in the darkness ..." *Ibid.*, pp. 10.

98   "Through a crude but ..." Bonazzi, *Man in the Mirror*, pp. 44.

98   "This seminal passage," *Ibid.*, pp. 43.

100   "I was prepared to walk ..." Griffin, in Fensch, pp. 112.

101   "Where you from?" Griffin, in Fensch, pp. 98.

102   "I developed a technique," Griffin, in Fensch, pp. 102.

103   Death threats in Mansfield, Texas, hung in effigy, in Fensch, pp. 107.

104   Klu Klux Klan beating, Fensch, 116.

105   Griffin illnesses, Fensch, 160-186.

105   "He died of everything," Fensch, pp. 186.

106   Publishing chronology in Fensch, pp. 211.

107   "continues to sell ..." Robert Bonazzi, e-mail to author, July 16, 2013.

Chapter 7

Page

108   "We continued through ..." Griffin, in Fensch, pp. 28.

109   He "was a football star ..." Vollers, *Ghosts of Mississippi*, pp. 34.

110   George Washington Carver coin, *Ibid.*, pp. 43.

111   Beckwith, Battle of Tarawa, *Ibid.*, pp. 27.

111   Beckwith marriage, *Ibid.*, pp. 29.

111   bitterness ..., *Ibid.*, pp. 30.

112   NAACP national leadership ... *Ibid.*, pp. 55.

113   "Report on Mississippi," *The Autobiography of Medgar Evers*, pp. 17.

116   Published death threats and "Hoover believed ..." Vollers, *Ghosts of Mississippi*, pp. 63.

117   Evers tributes, Wikipedia.

Chapter 8

Chapter 9

Page

128   "His public performances ..." Handler, in *The Autobiography of Malcolm X*, Grove Press paperback ed., 1966, pp. xii.

130   "no realistic goal for a nigger," Bruce Perry. *Malcolm: The Life of a Man Who Changed Black America*. Barrytown, N.Y.: Station Hill, 1991. pp. 42.

130   "Detroit Red ..." Chapter six in his autobiography is titled "Detroit Red."

130   "I want to get sent down South ...." *Autobiography of Malcolm X*, Grove Press paperback ed., pp. 106.

130   ... patterned after the Bastille, *Ibid.*, pp. 152.

131   Readings in prison, *Autobiography ...*, Grove Press paperback ed. pp. 175.

131   "Ten guards and ..." *Ibid.*, pp. 177.

131   Bend his knees and pray, *ibid.*, pp. 169.

131   "What's your alma mater?" *Ibid.*, 176.

131   "Between Mr. Muhammad's teachings ..." *Autobiography ...*, Grove Press (hardcover) ed., pp. 199, cited in Wikipedia.

131   "Ex-smoker. Ex-drinker." Goldman, *The Death and Life of Malcolm X*, pp. 46.

132 "No drinking, no smoking ..." *Ibid.*, pp. 19.

132 FBI file ..., Wikipedia and *The Death and Life of Malcolm X*, pp. 257, 259.

132 "Malcolm listened and learned ..." Goldman, pp. 54.

134 Spoke at Harvard, *Ibid.*, pp. 63.

134 "These aren't white people ..." and "Historically, I think ..." Malcolm X in Goldman, pp. 66.

135 "If you'll notice ..." Malcolm X in Goldman, pp. 71.

135 "How can anybody ..." Malcolm X, in Goldman, pp. 68.

136 "He is very articulate ..." Alex Haley, *Playboy* interview, January, 1965.

137 "Nothing but a circus ..." Malcolm X in Goldman, pp. 107.

137 Book contract, *Ibid.*, footnote, pp. 111.

137 "At the end ..." *Ibid.*, pp. 1.

138 Wounds found, Manning Marrable, *Malcolm X: A Life of Reinvention*, pp. 162, cited in Wikipedia.

138 Awards, Wikipedia

Chapter 10

Page

140   "I'm not a coward ..." King, quoted in Brinkley, *Rosa Parks: A Life*, pp. 133.

140   "As I thought further ..." King, *Stride Toward Freedom*, pp. 51.

142   "But there comes a time ..." *Ibid.*, pp. 69.

143   "... Montgomery's Negroes ..." *Ibid.*, pp. 89.

144   FBI suicide note, Kotz, Nick. *Judgment Days: Lyndon Baines Johnson, Martin Luther King, Jr. and the Laws that Changed America*, pp. 247. Also in Garrow, *Bearing the Cross*, pp. 373.

145   Notorious liar ... Burns, Roger. *Martin Luther King, Jr.: A Biography*, pp. 67.

145   FBI files, www.paperlessarchives.com

145   President Kennedy—picture made him "sick," Hansen, *The Dream*, pp. 12.

146   "Letter from the Birmingham Jail," in Washington, ed., *A Testament of Hope: The Essential Writings and Speeches of Martin Luther King, Jr.*, pp. 295, 301.

149   "One possibility ...," Hansen, *The Dream*, pp. 114.

149   "The Biblical ..." *Ibid.*, pp. 120.

150   "The police presence ..." *Ibid.*, pp. 32.

152   "The old-time Negro preacher ..." Johnson, quoted in Hansen, pp. 121.

153   "A nation that continues ..." King, quoted in Mary Susannah Robbins, *Against the Vietnam War: Writings by Activists*, pp. 109.

154   "Then I got to Memphis ..." King, in Simon Sebag Montefiore, *Speeches that Changed the World*, pp. 155.

155   "You cannot hear ..." Dyson, *April 4, 1968.* pp. 3.

156   "heart of a 60-year-old," PBS video "Citizen King."

156   King honors, Wikipedia.

157   King Center, Atlanta, www.thekingcenter.org.

Chapter 11

Page

159   "The title meant nothing ..." *Soul Sister*, Fawcett paper ed., pp. 15. (All subsequent quotations are from the Fawcett paperback ed.)

160   "He read it quietly ...," *Ibid.*, pp. 22.

161   *Esquire* magazine ... *Ibid.*, pp. 27.

161   "Might stay dark for a year ...," *Ibid.*, pp. 33.

161   "What about the medication ..." *Ibid.*, 42.

162   "In two or three weeks ..." *Ibid.*, pp. 44.

162   "I've packed all ...." *Ibid.*, pp. 60.

162   "I keep walking ..." *Ibid.*, pp. 63.

163   "It's not that the ...." *Ibid.*, pp. 63-64.

163   "I enter the Harlem Hospital ..." *Ibid.*, pp. 75.

164   Walk the streets with me ... *Ibid.*, pp. 77.

165   Harlem was ... like a cemetery ... *Ibid.*, pp. 130.

165   "First take a damp cloth ...," *Ibid.*, pp. 155.

165   Working like a nigger, *Ibid.*, pp. 156.

166   "Get yourself killed ...," *Ibid.*, pp. 219.

Chapter 12

Page

168   Assault sequence, Wikipedia and *Report of the Independent Commission on the Los Angeles Police Department.*

169   "hit his joints, hit his wrists ..." *Report of the Independent Commission on the Los Angeles Police Department*, 1991, pp. 7.

170   "Fractured facial bone" in Wikipedia, entry 1992 L.A. Riots

170   Sued Los Angeles, in Wikipedia, Rodney King entry.

170   "11 skull fractures ...." *Report of the Independent Commission*, pp. 8.

170   "intoxicated under California law ..." *Ibid.*, pp. 8.

170   Officers bragged ... *Ibid.*, pp. 15

170   Jury awards .... "Rodney King is Arrested after a Fight at His Home," *The Los Angeles Times/* Associated Press, Sept. 30, 2005.

170   Simi Valley jury members ..., Wikipedia (multiple sources).

171   "Can we all get along?" Mydans, Seth, "Jury Could Hear Rodney King Today," *The New York Times*, March 9, 1993.

172   George H.W. Bush, "Address to the Nation on the Civil Disturbances in Los Angeles, California," May 1, 1992.

172   Dead and injured in riots ... "The L.A. 53," *LA Weekly*, April 24, 2002.

173   Weeks after the rioting ... Oh, Hansook, "Destruction in 1992 L.A. Upheaval: How law enforcement let the largest urban riot/ rebellion rage on" cited in Wikipedia, 1992 Los Angeles Riots entry.

173   Federal civil rights trial verdicts, Mydans, Seth. "Verdict in Los Angeles: Fear Subsides with Verdict, But Residents Remain Wary," *The New York Times*, April 19, 1993.

173 "Nearly a quarter century ..." Wasserman in *Inside the L.A. Riots*, pp. 109.

175 Death of Rodney King .... "911 call reveals frantic moments, fiancee's pleas after finding Rodney King submerged in pool." *The Washington Post*, June 18, 2012 and Medina, Jennifer. "Police Beating Victim Who Asked 'Can We All Get Along?'" *The New York Times*, June 18, 2012.

Chapter 13

Page

176 New Caney ... for a decade, the author lived in Huntsville, Texas, and had a close personal friend who was a utilities company supervisor. She said that her crews *never* wanted to work in the New Caney area.

176 The current (2013) estimated population of New Caney, Texas, is 20,000. The current estimated population of Jasper, Texas, is 7,600.

176 "Deep east Texas ..." Temple-Raston, *A Death in Texas*, pp. 36.

178 "When I go ..." *A Death in Texas*, no pp., photo section caption.

179 Lighter and *Possum, Ibid.*, photo section caption.

180 Brewer and Rowles quotations, KHOU interview.

180 Rodman and Don King donations, in Paul Robinson, *Criminal Law, Case Studies & Controversies*, pp. 1176, cited in the James Byrd Jr. Wikipedia entry.

Chapter 14

Page

188 Zimmerman police trouble, NBC News March 27, 2012, cited in Wikipedia entry, The Shooting of Treyvon Martin.

190 Major companies resign from ALEC, "HP, Deere, CVS, MillerCoors, BestBuy Exit Controversial ALEC Post-Treyvon Martin Shooting," www.ibtimes.com, July 20, 2012.

A caveat to the reader: some users of Wikipedia have been skeptical of the accuracy of Wikipedia entries. In all cases, citations from Wikipedia in this book can also be "sourced" elsewhere.

Suggested Readings

Alexander, Michelle. *The New Jim Crow: Mass Incarceration in the Age of Colorblindness*. New York: The New Press, 2010.

Baldwin, James. *The Fire Next Time*. New York: The Dial Press, 1963.

Blow, Charles. "The Sadness Lingers." *The New York Times*, July 13, 2013.

Bonazzi, Robert. *Man in the Mirror: John Howard Griffin and the Story of Black Like Me*. Maryknoll, N.Y.: Orbis Books, 1997.

Booker, Simeon. *Shocking the Conscience: A Reporter's Account of the Civil Rights Movement*. Jackson, Ms.: The University Press of Mississippi, 2013.

Branch, Taylor. *Parting the Waters: America in the King Years*, 1954-63. New York: Simon and Schuster, 1988.

_____. *Pillar of Fire: America in the King Years, 1963-1965*. New York: Simon and Schuster, 1998.

_____. *At Canaan's Edge: American in the King Years, 1965-1968*. New York: Simon and Schuster, 2006.

Brinkley, Douglas. *Rosa Parks: A Life*. New York: Penguin Books, 2000.

Cone, James H. *Martin & Malcolm & America: A Dream or a Nightmare*. Maryknoll, N.Y.: Orbis Books, 2003.

Dyson, Michael Eric. *April 4, 1968: Martin Luther King, Jr.'s Death and How It Changed America*. New York: Basic Civitas Books, 2008.

_____. *I May Not Get There With You: The True Martin Luther King, Jr.* New York: The Free Press, 2000.

Emmett Till—the FBI Files. Filiquarian Publishing Co. (no city or year date listed. Available from Amazon www.Amazon.com)

Evers-Williams, Myrlie and Manning Marable. *The Autobiography of Medgar Evers: A Hero's Life and Legacy Revealed Through His Writings, Letters and Speeches*. New York: Basic Civitas Books, 2005.

Fensch, Thomas. *The Man Who Changed His Skin: The Life and Work of John Howard Griffin*. N. Chesterfield, Va.: New Century Books, 2011.

Fernandez, Manny. "Racial Tensions Flare Anew in a Texas Town." *The New York Times*, June 16, 2013.

Fishkin, Shelley Fisher. *Was Huck Black? Mark Twain and African American Voices*. New York: Oxford University Press, 1993.

Fox, Margolit. "Willie Louis, Who Named the Killers of Emmett Till at Their Trial, Dies at 76." *The New York Times*, July 24, 2013.

Friedly, Michael and David Gallen, eds. *Martin Luther King, Jr.—The FBI Files*. New York: Carroll and Graf, 1993.

Garrow, David J. *Bearing the Cross: Martin Luther King, Jr. and the Southern Christian Leadership Conference*. New York: William Morrow, 1986.

_____. *The FBI and Martin Luther King, Jr.: From "Solo" to Memphis*. New York: W.W. Norton Co., 1981.

Goldman, Peter. *The Death and Life of Malcolm X*. Urbana, Ill.: The University of Illinois Press, 1973.

Gregory, Dick. *Nigger: An Autobiography*. New York: Pocket Books, 1964.

Griffin, John Howard. *Black Like Me*. Boston: Houghton Mifflin, 1961. (Reprint eds., New York: Signet, 1962.)

Halberstam, David. *The Children*. New York: Random House, 1998.

Haley, Alex. "*Playboy* Interview—Dr. Martin Luther King, Jr.," *Playboy* magazine, January, 1965.

Halsell, Grace. *Soul Sister*. Cleveland: World Publishing Co., 1969. (reprint ed. New York: Fawcett, 1970.)

Hansen, Drew D. *The Dream: Martin Luther King, Jr. and the Speech That Inspired a Nation*. New York: Ecco/ HarperCollins, 2003.

Harris, James Henry. *The Forbidden Word: The Symbol and Sign of Evil in American Literature, History and Culture*. Eugene, Oregon: Cascade Books, 2012.

Hazen, Dan, ed. *Inside the L.A. Riots—What Really Happened—and Why It Will Happen Again*. New York: Institute for Alternative Journalism, 1992.

Hudson-Weems, Clenora. *Emmett Till: The Sacrificial Lamb of the Civil Rights Movement*. Bloomington, Ind., Author House, 1994.

Huie, William Bradford. *Wolf Whistle*. New York: Signet Books, 1959.

Hylton, Raymond P. "About V.U.U.—History." Virginia Union University website: www.VUU.edu

Kaplan, Justin. *Mr. Clemens and Mark Twain: A Biography*. New York: Simon and Schuster, 1990.

King, Martin Luther, Jr. *Stride Toward Freedom: The Montgomery Story*. New York: Harper & Row, 1958.

_____. *Why We Can't Wait*. New York: Harper & Row, 1964.

Lauber, John. *The Making of Mark Twain: A Biography*. New York: Farrar, Strauss & Giroux, 1985.

Miller, Doug. "James Byrd's killer: 'I'd do it all over again'" Houston KHOU television interview, Sept. 20, 2011.

Mills, Kay. *This Little Light of Mine: The Life of Fannie Lou Hamer*. New York: Dutton, 1993.

Noble, William. *Bookbanning in America: Who Bands Books?—and Why*. Middlebury, Vt., Paul S. Eriksson, Publisher, 1990.

Oates, Stephen B. *Let the Trumpet Sound: The Life of Martin Luther King, Jr*. New York: Harper & Row, 1982.

Parks, Rosa and James Haskins. *Rosa Parks: My Story*. New York: Dial Books, 1992.

Parks, Rosa and Gregory J. Reed. *Quiet Strength: The Faith, the Hope, and the Heart of a Woman Who Changed a Nation*. Grand Rapids: Zondervan, 1994.

Perry, Bruce. *Malcolm: The Life of a Man Who Changed Black America*. Barrytown, N.Y., Station Hill, 1991.

Pollack, Harriet and Christopher Metress, eds. *Emmett Till In Literary Memory and Imagination.* Baton Rouge: Louisiana State University Press, 2008.

Sprigle, Ray. *In the Land of Jim Crow.* New York: Simon & Schuster, 1949.

Steinbeck, John. *The Grapes of Wrath.* New York: The Viking Press, 1939.

Temple-Raston, Dina. *A Death in Texas: A Story of Race, Murder, and a Small Town's Struggle for Redemption.* New York: Henry Holt, 2002.

Theoharis, Jeanne. *The Rebellious Life of Rosa Parks.* Boston: The Beacon Press, 2013.

Till-Mobley, Mamie and Christopher Benson. *Death of Innocence: The Story of the Hate Crime that Changed America.* New York: Random House, 2003.

Tucker, Abigail. "Digging up the Past at a Richmond Jail." *Smithsonian* magazine, March 2009.

Twain, Mark. *The Adventures of Huckleberry Finn.* New York: Book of the Month Club edition, 1992.

_____. *Life on the Mississippi.* New York: Book of the Month Club edition, 1992.

Vollers, Maryanne. *Ghosts of Mississippi: The Murder of Medgar Evers, the Trials of Byron De La Beckwith, and the Haunting of the New South.* Boston: Little, Brown, 1995.

Washington, James M., ed. *A Testament of Hope: The Essential Writings and Speeches of Martin Luther King, Jr.* San Francisco: Harper San Francisco, 1986.

Whitfield, Stephen J. *A Death in the Delta: The Story of Emmett Till*. New York: The Free Press, 1988. (Reprint ed. Baltimore: The Johns Hopkins University Press, 1991.)

Wilkerson, Isabel. *The Warmth of Other Suns: The Epic Story of America's Great Migration*. New York: Random House, 2010.

Woodward, C. Vann. *The Strange Career of Jim Crow*. New York: Oxford University Press, 1974.

X, Malcolm. *The Autobiography of Malcolm X*. New York: Grove Press, 1965.

Index

About the author ...

THOMAS FENSCH has always had a passion for the printed word.

He has published the only full-length biography of John Howard Griffin: *The Man Who Changed His Skin: the Life and Work of John Howard Griffin* (2011) and has also published five books about John Steinbeck. He has an international reputation in Steinbeck scholarship.

Additionally, he has published books about: Theodor "Dr. Seuss" Geisel; Ernest Hemingway; James Thurber; Oskar Schindler and a variety of other nonfiction books.

He has a doctorate from Syracuse University and is on the faculty of Virginia Union University, Richmond.

Fensch lives outside Richmond with his four veteran literary advisors: Sally, a Great Pyrenees; Wolfie, a white German Shepherd; Charlie, a Labradoodle and Miss Gypsy, a Goldendoodle.